Martia

by

Karl William Marx Sr., B.A., M.S., Ph.D.

This is a book about a real American, Louisiana-born Cajun, Bayou Swamp and Street Fighting system. It may look like Karate, Jiu Jitsu, Kickboxing, or other Fighting Arts, but it isn't.

Dare To Learn. I DARE YOU!

Caution! This book is not for the faint hearted

Read at your own risk.

Your life will be affected one way or another

First Edition

Printed on acid-free paper

Library of Congress Control No: 2004091483

ISBN 0-9746336-2-3

Fifth Estate 03/04

Introduction

Dear Reader,

In September 1978, I first met Karl William Marx, Sr. There was nothing unusual about the meeting; however I knew the moment I met him that he was an exceptional person! He had something special to say.   I knew both of these things, although I had just met him. Later I learned why I had these two reactions.

He enrolled in one of my classes here at Northwestern State University of Louisiana. Since as a teacher I wanted to know each of my students as well as possible, learned more about Grand Master Marx. He and I had many talks in which he shared with me many tenets of his philosophy and his many theories concerning martial arts and its relationship to life.

Grand Master Marx is a thinker, a doer, and above all a humanitarian who has a deep concern for each individual with whom he comes into contact. He is a deeply emotional man who is "aware" of almost everything and everyone around him. He is a counselor who is never too busy to listen, who is concerned, and who empathizes (one of the most difficult things to do).   In these days of "hurry, scurry," these things make Grand Master Marx an exceptional person; however, remember I said he also had something special to say.

As our teacher-student relationship blossomed into a friendship, Grand Master Marx began to share, in addition to our talks, some of his writings, most of which were letters to his student friend and colleague, Mark Steven Williams. I was amazed and impressed! I was intrigued by much of what he had shared in these letters. In addition, I reviewed most of his writing he had accumulated over a seven-year period.

Grand Master Marx had been advised to publish this material and met with many difficulties in trying to accomplish this feat. Finally, he enlisted my assistance. To tell the truth, I was most honored that he felt he could trust me to help him because I had very little knowledge of his field (martial arts) and the school of martial arts (Keichu-Do) he had founded. However, remember, I told you that I thought he had something special to say, and I wanted him to be able to say it in such a way that others would listen (read).

Therefore, my task was undertaken humbly and enthusiastically. Grand Master Marx and I spent hour after hour reading, discussing, organizing, sharing, debating, etc. After many hours, painstaking hours, this book that is that "baby" Grand Master Marx conceived many years ago, carried for a seven-year gestation period, and finally borne after a long period of labor.

This book is presented in the form of letters to Mark S. Williams. I have edited each letter; however, Grand Master Marx's style and meaning have not been changed. I know you will enjoy reading each letter because he writes as if he were sitting next to you and talking with you. However, you will not have the privilege of being able to discuss the various ideas he presents as I did.

In this his first book (I know there will be others because he has so much to say), Grand Master Marx introduces Keichu-Do and its teachings.   This book contains eight chapters.

- **Chapter 1** gives a broad introduction and forms a base for the understanding of Keichu-Do.

- **Chapter 2** relates the basic philosophy of Keichu-Do; however, as you know no one can separate or detach philosophy from any chapter in this book.

- **Chapter 3** deals with mind power and its importance. Grand Master Marx introduces what he calls "mental attacks."

- **Chapter 4** discusses the renowned Ki or Chi, the force behind mind power.

- **Chapter 5** reveals behavioral aspects of Keichu-Do.

- **Chapter 6** explains causes and symptoms of mental attacks.

- **Chapter 7** discloses ideas involving human effort in relation to our minds and bodies.

- **Chapter 8** involves a Grand Master's admonition to his student of their responsibilities in human development.

Enjoy your journey through this book. Do not feel guilty if you get the feeling you are "peeping over the shoulder" of Grand Master Marx as you read each letter.

Above all, be on guard against the daily mental attacks!

With deep Makato,

Thomas A. Clinton, Ph.D.

Acknowledgments

To the authors of all my research materials, I give my thanks and gratitude. I have attempted to name all of you, and to give credit where it is due. If I have missed anyone please let me know and I will acknowledge you in the sequel to this publication.

To my past mentor in graduate school for my Master of Science degree, a true friend, Thomas A. Clinton, Ph.D., my thesis might not have passed if not for your influence.

To Shihan Linda McCoy Carrie 6th Dan. (Big Mack) Keichu's very first Grand Champion, and the highest ranked woman as of this date, in Keichu, you were a really great best friend. I thank you for all the faithful and loyal years you dedicated to Keichu. Also you're still the **only** person in the World to have ever literally kicked my butt, Ha! Remember?

To Peter Urban for your influence from your own book, "The Dojo" Gosh! I hope I have the correct name for you book. Fellows like us should be on closer terms. I regret not having the honor of ever meeting you in person.

To Maximillian De La Croix, the sharpest intellectual I ever knew. I wonder where you are today. 11/19/03. Be blessed little Brother.

To Mark S. Williams, I just wish I had been a better role model for you and the others. You were like a son to me. You helped me to build Keichu, you were my **Uki**, and felt the success of every technique I put together. However dear Mark, you were **Not the SOKE!**

Disclaimer

It has been about 24 years since I began work on this book. My life has changed a lot in that time. I have matured a great deal in my Christian walk and even became ordained as an Evangelist Pastor. A lot of this was written at a time of my not really knowing enough about my responsibilities as a Christian. Much of this treatise was written concerning not particularly Christian literature, but many Occult beliefs... Perfect Liberty, Silva Mind Control, and others.

That aside, there is a great deal of truth in most of this work. In many places I have rewritten and changed words and placed the correct Christian explanation. Some of you might find parts that are not of your particular denomination, and some might be offended, I pray not. Others may find your minds stretched to the limit with information not yet known or accepted by the public, or media. There is some HEAVY brain input here, if you find something you feel is unbiblical, disregard it. If you don't agree, that doesn't mean you're correct. Let the Bible be your guide.

Karl Marx, Sr. - Martial Art Spirit

Special Acknowledgements

To my lovely wife Kathleen "Kathy" Marx, without her encouragement I would not have started this book again. My son Dustin who is so helpful like his mother in teaching Keichu at our Academy. To Jeff Martinez whose loyalty and hard practice made him a two time World Karate Champion! To my loyal black belts Heather and Travis who have been with me since my first class in the back room of the K.G.D.P. Christian Radio Station, in 1974. To the Sanchez Family, Heidi, Daniel, David and Rose. They were my first World Champions since coming to Santa Maria, aside from Ryan Case. To the fabulous Prewett family whose support, hard work, generous blessings have been my most appreciated benefactors - not to mention the fact that they have three World Champions amongst them. The Crothers Family - Dennis, Linda and Jeffery - who are like my own children, Mom and Dad included; Jeff Crothers being the winningest Keichu Karate Champion in Keichu history. His dad Dennis is the over-50 division world record holder, the oldest Keichu man to win a World title, and on the same day as his son. My hat is off to Danny Gilliland, 6th Dan Orthodox Keichu-Ryu, who has to be the best Keichu instructor in the world, by the fact that he has more World champion students than even I do. I am not about to acknowledge all the people who deserve an "atta boy," or pat on the back, however I cannot leave out Eldridge "Cricket" Conley, 7th Dan, the highest ranked Keichu black belt in the World, and his Number 1 student, German National, and World Champion Patrick Paolozzi. Oh! And I can't forget the man who did all my typing for this book, Mr. Matthew Hickman. This young man is mostly responsible for his encouraging effort in typing so quickly.

Last but certainly not the least, my very special son and heir to Keichu-Do, Vaughn Victor Marx, and his entire staff and family.

TABLE OF CONTENTS

Page

Number

Martial Art Spirit

By

Karl William Marx Sr., B.A., M.S., Ph.D.

CHAPTER 1 - JANUARY 10, 1974

Dear Sensei Mark S. Williams,

In this, first of many letters, I will write about the similarities of Keichu-Ryu and other martial arts. Sensei, you have requested that I write my lectures in letter form and mail them to you for present and future publication.

I will attempt to write you as often as time will allow. This my first letter will be an introduction to facilitate your understanding of Keichu-Do—my feelings concerning what a Dojo and a Sensei should be in regards to teaching Keichu-Do Karate-Do.

As you are aware, my field is in self defense, philosophy, and other areas of martial arts that are not commonly taught at the Dojos throughout the world. I only hope that what I have to say will one day be available to anyone who can benefit from it.

Keichu-Do's origins do not date back to over 2,000 years or even four or five hundred years. It is not lost in mythical legends or handed down from generation to generation in close family ties. Keichu has always been in existence since man began. It was the first law of nature in God's Divine Plan. "Devoting oneself entirely" to God, nature and self-preservation. The name was not the same but the idea was always there in truth. So you see, my son, I will not claim any particular great ancestor-ship with the old masters of the past. When we use our imagination we see some similarities in nature, Oriental religions and the martial arts. When you know me, you observe Oriental thought process in philosophy. I am a minister of Jesus Christ the only way, and I am of course, in the martial arts.

Why did I start teaching a martial art primarily for women? Why did I choose the name Keichu? And why am I into Christianity and the martial arts? It is not really important. What is important is what I am doing now in this time and space. If one is looking for creditability, I feel I am as qualified as did any of the others who founded their own styles and taught their particular favorite philosophy.

If one wants to build a family tree, let's start with this one, for example.

- <u>Nippon-No Goshin Jitsu</u>   500 B.C.
- <u>Seiyo No Goshin Jitsu</u>   1200 A.D.
- <u>Beikoku-No-Goshin Jitsu</u>   1400 A.D
- <u>Shinshiki-Go-Do</u>   1600 A.D.
- <u>Keichu-Ryu Ju-Jitsu</u>   1960-American
- <u>Keichu Karate-Do</u>   1972
- <u>Hoshin-Jitsu-Ryu Ju-Jitsu</u>   1979
- <u>Kindai-Gaku Kobudo Jutsu Kai</u>   1980
- <u>Fudoshin-Ryu</u>   1981

But what does it really all mean? To study Keichu is to know a little of Keichu, to be a student of Keichu is to search for truth through Keichu. More importantly is the fact. That to know Jesus, one should search for the truth in the holy bible. Christ is the way the truth and the life, as well as the light, that covers enlightenment.

Keichu-Do is a martial art, not unlike Karate, Tae-Kwon-Do and others. It is a concept, a way of life. Karate and Tae-Kwon-Do have until recently been relatively unknown to most of the world's population; only in the past two decades have Americans become aware of these fascinating arts of self-defense. By means of television and motion pictures, a new hero image has been

3

implanted in the American mind. No longer is man's strength limited to the weapon he carries; he now possesses the weaponless weapon, his own body. Perhaps the most significant result of the growing awareness of martial arts is the realization among educators that here is an unexplored area of knowledge. There is much to be learned about Karate-Keichu-Do and Tae-Kwon-Do as practical means of self defense, as sports, and as philosophies.

American parents have become aware of the necessity of equipping their children with knowledge of the martial arts to develop them fully, mentally as well as physically. One of the great problems facing American society today is lack of respect for authority; it has become common for some young people to harass policemen and teachers. Since a child's respect for an adult often has strength as its basis, it is essential that all adults who deal with children be physically competent. The youngster who is reared in an atmosphere of shootings and knifings would perhaps emerge from childhood as a better citizen if, as a youth, he felt respect for those in authority. After all, who respects anyone who has to use a club or gun in a situation where it could or might have been avoided?

I believe if martial arts were to be made a natural part of one's education, much of the unhappiness and neurosis so prevalent today would disappear; crime would inevitably be reduced the taboo against physically trained women would be lifted, and the defenseless women of today would be capable of defending themselves in any situation. Teaching girls from the sixth grade through high school would certainly reduce the crime of rape after a few hundred thousand women black belts graduated and became a part of the community.

Americans who served in the Far East during World War II and the Korean War introduced Karate and other martial arts to the United States. Since then, thousands of Americans have adopted the martial arts whole-heartedly as a way of life, as a means of self defense, for the competition or sport, or simply as a rewarding physical development program.

This letter is intended to introduce a new form of self-defense which should have been taught all along but was somehow neglected. Keichu-Do is the system that teaches mental self-defense which, in my opinion, is more important than its physical counterpart. After all, if the mind is not functioning properly, the body cannot carry out the techniques anyway. Martial arts are filling two vital needs in American society: the human need to express emotion, and to live without fear.

Americans, taught from childhood to suppress their feelings, often acquire psychological problems. Through a martial art such as Karate, Tae-Kwon-Do, or Keichu-Do, young people find an outlet for aggression, and learn not to fear emotions and feel free to express themselves by being more assertive. Countless college students are studying martial arts, keenly aware of its usefulness throughout life.

Having realized the value of the martial arts, increasing numbers of police academies and military posts are using its techniques. Physicians too have become well aware of the value of using martial arts as prescription therapy for many of their patients.

Over the years evidence has proven that those who practice some form of martial art are rarely ill and are generally more vigorous than the average person. Not only do martial arts training improve one's health physically, it also benefits ones mental attitude.

Martial arts training are based on rigid discipline, a factor which limits the number of students who will ever achieve high proficiency. Certain types of people can never make it. They are quitters. That is why black belts are so highly respected; only an exceptional person can reach this revered level.

Karate societies and organizations, as well as societies dedicated to other martial arts, are springing up all over America, Europe and Asia, filling the social needs of individuals and communities alike. Despite its competitiveness, martial arts training develop a feeling of brotherhood among its adherents; great rapport soon exists between brothers and sisters.

The training hall or Dojo is a lodge, a home for the devoted. It opens many other worlds to students; the world of self-confidence where fear has no place. The martial arts was once considered an esoteric Oriental subject of unknown origin whose main requirement was that its practitioners beat parts of their bodies on inanimate objects for the purpose of developing hardened limbs and the ability to destroy things.

While this is correct of some extremists, this barbaric Karate-man is an absurdity, for the martial arts philosophy of calmness, humility, respect, and confidence is the antithesis of aggression and inhumanity to man.

Instruction in the martial arts is one of the newest professions to evolve in the social structure and can be a very rewarding field of endeavor. Full-time or part-time instructors can make a very good living teaching this way of life; and if not for the monetary gains, for the joy of seeing young students become champions or just better people is fantastic and rewarding enough. This information is thanks to Peter Urban's book, <u>The Dojo</u>.

Martial arts are taught in various places, depending upon the instructor. Some are taught in YMCA buildings, living rooms, garages, back yards etc, but most commonly, martial arts are taught in some kind of school: Dojo for Karate, Dojong for Tae-Kwon-Do, or Kwoon for Kung Fu. Taking information from Grandmaster Peter Urban's book, The Karate Dojo, I will give you his definition: "Karate is taught in a school called Dojo. More than merely a gymnasium or club, a Dojo is a cherished place of learning and brotherhood for Martial Artist devotees. But the word 'Dojo' implies an even broader meaning; to the dedicated student, the Dojo soon becomes a concept, a way of life. The word is symbolic of the methodological, the ideological, the philosophical aspects of Martial Arts."

Keichu-Do, like Karate and Tae-Kwon-Do, is one aspect of the martial arts, a collective system of the training of the mind and the body according to certain principles. The principles vary with each of the many systems - Karate, Kenpo, Keichu, Kung Fu, Tai-Chi-Chuan, Judo, Jiu-Jitsu, Bo-jitsu, Aikido, Tae-Kwon-Do, and Kendo are examples of such systems. Karate, translated as "empty hand", and Keichu as "devoting oneself entirely", deal primarily in developing the body so as to bring about a practiced control of the limbs and in developing certain mental energies (sometimes called "Ki","Kime", or "Chi") to make the body into a highly effective tool of the mind; the body becomes in effect a weaponless weapon.

As you know, Mark, the mental demands in rigorous Keichu training are more taxing than the physical demands. Although the term "Martial Arts" means fighting arts, a truer interpretation of its Oriental meaning may be found in the Japanese word "Budo," which freely translated, implies "the way of the fighter." The suffix "Do" or "Way", which is often used in the Orient, and by the Chinese "Tao", does not mean only the learning and application of physical techniques and skills. Its meaning is more profound; the mental and spiritual use of the techniques and the integration of these techniques are all-important.

A "way" or "path" is intended to lead the individual to the attainment of perfection or what is often known as self-realization, enlightenment, or simple maturity in Christ Jesus. Because of this spiritual attitude, which was encountered, nurtured and grown to flower in the Dojo, a real martial artist never gives up, quits or asks for mercy; they are incapable of squirming in the face of death. They are able to respond to conditions around them with objectivity and calm detachment, even while being intimately involved in them

You know, Mark, the highest achievement for a martial artist is the attainment of virtue. The hallmarks of this virtue are relaxation, even-mindedness, esteem in self-confidence, graciousness, humility, courage, consideration of others, to name a few.

Martial arts can be considered as a philosophy based on the belief that a sound mind is achieved through the development of a virtuous character and a sound body is achieved through rigorous training. The natural result of sound mind and sound body is oneness. Many martial artists believe that learning and excellence cannot stand still. They believe the standards of excellence wherein to excel is the common goal of all or should be at least. They increase their efforts and raise their goals as each step toward excellence is achieved.

Their martial arts training is reflected in every aspect of their daily living. As they train their bodies to make them stronger and healthier, they develop their characters accordingly. They, then, transcend the limits of the physical.

The origin of martial arts was the development of a way to free the ego from the limitations of physical equality. A traditional Dojo is, in sense, a patriarchy. The "Sensei" is the master of the Dojo. "Sensei" is the Japanese word for "honorable teacher". The true Sensei regards his or her students as his many sons and daughters, seeing them as they can never see themselves. He affects the development of their bodies and characters—this is the responsibility of his or her art. The Dojo is sometimes the home of the Sensei; students come to his home to learn his way of life.

The Sensei

A Sensei must always be an example of high virtue. The relationships with the many students must be, above all, objective and well defined. Only in this way is there perceptual learning and improvement. Since all martial arts training are primarily oriented towards the spirit of self-reliance, the Sensei has an obligation to set an example for the students in all things in excellence, discipline, moderation, and wisdom.

A Sensei thoroughly learns the art of helping himself or herself before obtaining the ability to help others. Often in the course of training, a student reaches a standstill in development due to excessive   ambition, importance, fear of failure, or for other emotional and psychological reasons.

According to the situation, the Sensei is then required to become a counselor or friend, as well as a teacher, in order to help the student solve his or her own problem. Over-training is just as profitless as under-training: too much effort is an indication that the student might have lost faith in himself; lack of effort is identified with giving up.

The Sensei gives recognition and confidence when deserved, strong honest criticism when necessary. Most Sensei are somewhat perfectionists; thus, compliments are few unless necessary in the Dojo.

Students learn to take for granted the fact that the basic requirement for continued development is to put forth their utmost effort at all times. Maintaining their bodies in the best shape and physical condition possible is mandatory for all students. They learn to practice autosuggestion and meditation. They learn that "winners never quit and quitters never win."

Professor Richard Kim once said, "It is the challenge that makes lifetime devoters of the art." The challenge is from oneself and to oneself. All martial arts Dojos should have time allotted for the practice of prayer and meditation. In some, it precedes and ends the training sessions; in others it is practiced only at the end of training. It takes time to develop the ability to clear the mind completely of all thoughts at will. It is difficult at first to think of nothing but Jesus. Some students start by concentrating on a mental picture that is easy to imagine; often they choose the image of a light bulb. With the eyes closed, the student concentrates on remembering how a lighted bulb looks. The body is relaxed in a comfortable position. By concentrating only on the mental image, one finds it easier to exclude all other thoughts. This is a beginning technique; eventually the practice of meditation techniques leads one to the ability to clear the mind and relax the body instantly.

Many college students testify to the beneficial effect of their practice of meditation when they have examinations; they find themselves able to clear their minds of all worries and nervousness before they start their test.

Imagine that you are entering a Dojo for the first time. The following is typical of what you could expect to see. When the clock strikes the hour, the senior student (highest ranking student) signals the beginning of formal training. The students quickly form ranks, standing close together in a militaristic posture. Suddenly, not a sound can be heard. Everyone drops smartly to the floor in the formal sitting position and awaits the coming of the Sensei. Their attitude is alert when he approaches his place. The higher the rank of the teacher, the more elaborate the formalities. Depending on the teachers rank in the system, his students call him or her "Sensei" or "Shihan" (pronounced she-hon), which denotes "teacher" and "professor," respectively. The young masters are respected, but the old masters are venerated.

The Belt System

The martial arts method of evaluating merit and development is know as the belt system, with the color of the belts designating the various steps of attainment. In Karate the system is divided into two simple categories; the lower level is called "Kyu," implying the idea of "boy" or "girl"; the upper level is called "dan," implying the idea of "man" or "woman."

As a student of the martial arts develops physically, he or she is expected to broaden his/her character accordingly. The requirements for each level vary in each style or system and in each Dojo according to the Sensei's standards.

The white belt denotes the beginner. There are usually three steps which students must attain before they can attain the next belt level. A good student is able to successfully complete the requirements after three or four months of intensive training. The qualifications include excellence in the following: primary physical conditioning, standard training procedure of the style being studied, basic fighting forms, and training dances or Katas. The students are motivated to do well by a status system; they see that the color of the belt changes as their abilities and accomplishments increase.

So it is with Keichu-Ryu, Mark. I'll write more in my next correspondence.

Remember; keep Jesus Christ first, in all you do.

Soke Marx

CHAPTER 2 - JUNE 4, 1974

Dear Mark,

Today I will write to you about the philosophy of Keichu-Do. I hope from this letter you will have a better understanding of Keichu-Do, its purpose and goals, and the reason I feel so strongly about teaching mankind this way of life.

As I told you in my previous letter, Keichu-Do involves both mental and spiritual aspects of martial arts. Keichu's philosophy is the essence or difference between Keichu and the other forms and systems of Karate, Kung Fu, etc. The mental aspect of Keichu's philosophy was founded many years ago in Japan. One of the earliest founders of this way of life was Master Tokumitsu Kanada, who taught Master Tokuharu Miki, the Father of the present Spiritual Supreme Grand Master whom we call Oshieoya-sama, Tokuchika Miki.

Oshieoya-sama is one of the world's greatest living philosophers and is also a greatly religious man. In fact, he is a member of the Council of Religious Corporations under the Ministry of Education. In the literary world he is well known as an essayist, poet and publisher. Some of his works became Japan's best selling books and remained so for some time. His poetry is published regularly in the monthly literary magazines. He is also the publisher of the Geijutsu Seikatsu, Japan's leading magazine of the fine arts. These are but a few of his many great accomplishments. So you can see why we feel toward Keichu the way we do. It is, not just an art or self-defense system; it is truly a whole, everyday living way of life for me and hopefully for my disciples and students. (I was involved in this cult as a minister, until Christ Jesus brought me back to reality).

The original name of this cult organization was Hito-no-michi. On September 29, 1946, Tokuchika Miki re-established a temple on the island of Kyushu. Shortly after he renamed the system Shin-no-jiyu, which translated means "Perfect Liberty". This however, covered only two –thirds of self-defense, the mental and spiritual aspects. While Shin-no-jiyu did have a physical part it was mostly expressive in art forms of poetry, painting, golf, flower arrangements, and Kendo teams.

In 1960 I was inspired to create another aspect of life, through physical exercise and self-defense in the forms of Jiu-Jitsu and Karate. Utilizing my many years' experience in self-defense, I created Keichu.

Mark, while I do not claim that the techniques in Keichu are superior to other forms, I do contend that at least they are very practical and effective, more so than many others I have studied from afar and witnessed. And most important, Keichu offers a philosophy that most other systems fail to teach. Oh, it's true some styles or disciplines do teach some philosophy, but do not be deceived by some inadequate philosophy, which may claim to have the ultimate, final and universal answer to problems of mankind. I have learned that Jesus Christ is in fact the ultimate and only way. We offer people the opportunity to understand the correct mental attitudes in accord with God's will.

Then how does a person perceive this correct attitude, which is in accordance with the Holy Bible? And why is it so important to attain a correct mental state? Man's first step toward the answer is to realize that Christ is the Way. Yes, Son, your life is a continuous work of study because each and every action of your life from cradle to grave, involves self-expression. But before further elaboration, let us look into the overall teaching of Keichu.

Now since Keichu translated means "devoting One's Self entirely," we mean to God, and mankind. Like religion, Keichu believes that God is the center or essence of Life, Ki or Chi "as it were" and we receive all our forces, energy, Ki, etc, from the center force, "God." The concept of deity and the metaphysical basis of any mature religion are complex subjects, but I would like to explain here that Keichu is not a religion per se, but a way of life which could be called technically a religion by anyone who wanted to do so. But this is not the purpose for its beginning. What I want to explain is the relationship Keichu has to mankind, nature, the universe and most importantly, God.

In Keichu, Mark, as you already know, our definition or view of God is that of a monotheistic nature. God can be called Abba Father. But the name is of little importance, for we believe the Judeo-Christian God, embraces everything—good, beauty, ugliness, people, truth, happiness, misfortune,--in short, all things are nestled in Him. God is that power and love, which embraces all, creates all, nurtures all and makes things progress and develop. Also very important, incidentally, is that we must realize that all things progress and develop according to the will of God, for here are the answers to some of the questions regarding mans birth and death.

Mark, we must also comprehend that God created all things and made them in mutual relationship to one another. Red is red because we recognize colors other than red. Good-bad, fast-slow, high-low, man-woman, etc, all become meaningful because we recognize them in relationship to one another. The relativity of all things is one of the most remarkable aspects of God's creation.

And, of course man's existence is always this relativity. Someone might ask you, what then, is the nature of man? And what is his relationship with God? Well, we believe that man is a manifestation of God. But, make no mistakes, God is not MAN, and man is not God Himself. Man remains man to the end. He is merely one of the countless things created by God. But Man alone possesses the body, intellect, individuality, and above all the desire for artistic expression. From cradle to grave, Man lives his life by expressing himself. At times, self-expression results in an epoch-making event, but normally, Man expresses himself and his individuality in ordinary everyday tasks. Since self-expression is mans birth endowment, man dies when his self-expression comes to an end.

Understand this, Mark; Man's unique position is not unconditional. Life is but a small hole in eternity. Before birth, eternity...beyond death, another eternity. While the nature of God is to be eternal, entire, unlimited, Man is but a limited, circumscribed, and conditional phenomenon. The life of Man is a constant struggle between his inevitable limitations and his desire for the unlimited. Man's limitations are apparent in his intellectual abilities, physical capabilities, and spiritual perception. What makes Man the superior of all creatures is his conscious desire to overcome these limitations. Thus, humans have formed societies to benefit from the accumulated knowledge of people in the past and present.

Man's accomplishments in the field of science and technology have surpassed the wildest visions of his ancestors. The progress and development of human society can, in essence, be attributed to Man's boundless desire for human expression. Furthermore, life is made pleasant and interesting because Man has this desire for expression because he feels joy and satisfaction from his endeavors to manifest this desire. Man is noble because he has individuality. But "No man is an island." Human society is multifarious, many-hued and full of

16

indescribable charm because a multitude of unique individuals express themselves in a complex way, woven together like the most exquisite figured brocade. Man is a social being. Man and society are never mutually exclusive. Man can freely express his own individuality by working upon the whole of creation, but his self-expression should not become a hindrance to others or bring misfortune on society.

The joy of self-expression through Kata is a joy which can be felt only when there are other people who appreciate, utilize, and welcome one's acts. A joy shared with others becomes a joy twice blessed. But how can a natural expression of self, you may wonder, help but be selfish or self-centered? The answer is simple: Your natural self-expression cannot be selfish if you have a clear understanding of your relative position with your fellow man, society, God, and the Divine Trinity. When Man's self-expression is not in accordance with the Holy Trinity, the result is sickness, or misfortune of some kind, at least in many cases.

In Keichu we teach our students to regard the results of egoistic expression as a divine warning and call it "mishirase" or "the wicked shall not go unpunished." They are in a way welcomed as an opportunity to discover the faults or mental habits which are contrary to the scheme of God. So in our minds even misfortunes have value. But you must remember that buffeting "mishirase" is not always God's punishment, nor are always blessings rewards. God has bestowed on Man the ability to freely express himself. Blessings and "mishirase" are merely phenomena of Our Lord's Plan, which are readily comprehensible to man. It is the interpretation of Man that gives positive or negative values to these phenomena. Therefore, Man's life can be said to be a struggle to overcome his limitations. His desire for money, faster promotions, a happier life are common examples of Man's struggle against his temporary or inherent limitations. For the child, the sense of limitation is almost nonexistent.

However the process of growing eventually replaces the dreams, fantasies, and confidence with a sober realization of serious limitations. Is it possible to free ourselves from the agony, misery, and frustration of such a depressing realization? Christ, in the broadest sense, and Keichu are answers. Life must be lived with a Christ-like mind. And life will be truly artistic <u>when we have a correct Christ-like attitude toward life</u>. Keichu is not an escape. It is a constructive and positive step forward. We instruct our students to come to Keichu, not with selfish reasons of becoming black belts, but instead to discover how they can contribute to the eternal peace and welfare of mankind, while finding happiness for themselves by attaining a state of mind where both they and others become blessed through freely, positively, and pleasantly expressing their true unique individuality.

Mark, you must teach Keichu as I have taught you, changes can be made, but only with my first being able to see and make sure that the change will benefit Keichu.

Remember in all you do keep Jesus Christ first. With love

Grand Master Marx

CHAPTER 3, PART 1 - December 10, 1974

Dear Mark,

In my last two letters to you, I discussed Keichu-Do philosophy; this time I will write about the power of the mind, mental attacks and their effects on the human body.

In your letter to me you requested I write a thesis or something similar to let others know my thoughts. This letter is intended to answer your request. My information and thoughts come from many years of study and reading many good works by great authors, and some not so great, but who had interesting things to say and write about. Have you ever been asked, "What do you want the most out of life?" Peace of mind, health, long life, or financial success?

Well, the truth is, many of us can have not only one of these dreams come true but all of the. The secret (if you want to use the term as such) or the answer could be gained by unlocking the power of our minds. The farthest reaches of man's imagination have brought him to the thresholds of discovery of the very secrets of the universe. But has man really come close to topping those secrets or has he, in his own stubborn way, actually veered away from that discovery?

I say some have come close and others have gone astray because they refrain from learning from those who know. This foolish pride prevents them from advancing to higher mental levels because they believe they are already great, and their learning stops advancing; thus, they stagnate and never reach their fullest potentials. God's great gift to Man is a mind, soul and brain, not necessarily in that order. Anyway, Mark, man's brain, as you know, is a bundle of nerves and tissues that weigh only about two percent of his body weight. It rests delicately packaged inside the cranium and is the key to many things. It only remains for those willing enough to explore, to investigate, to pursue, and to unlock the great secrets embodied in Man himself. Modern man is believed to be the highest pinnacle in God's Divine Plan. I see human evolution in three progressive stages: physical, mental, and spiritual.

Human progress depends entirely upon individual and collective effort. However, there are other less fortunate individuals who despite their intellectual advancement and cultural attainments, have not yet succeeding in discarding the destructive traits or in inhibitions of his primitive forebears. Because of these learned and instinctive urges, beliefs, and thought processes, millions of humans are periodically and permanently ill in mind and body. This is largely due to too much reliance on self and too little on God, God has, I believe, endowed everyone with latent powers capable of making them healthy, wealthy, and wise if someone else doesn't mess up their chance at birth or before(drug abuse). Christ admitted "greater things that these will you do."

Christ came primarily to show many the way to spiritual attainment through mental development. This is salvation. He did many wonders to demonstrate the potential powers inherent in human nature, including the power to heal. I personally believe that we all have consummated geniuses inside us. Some appear to have it more than others, and the awareness or unawareness of it is what makes each of us into masters or holds down to mediocrity. I think mediocrity is self inflicted and that genius is self bestowed, at least to a degree.

Walter Russell, founder of the University of Science and Philosophy, said, "The key which unlocks awareness and lets in the universal power that makes man a master is desire; when it is released into the great eternal energy of the universe." Sounds a little too much like Bruce Lee doesn't it?

Mark, the real essentials of greatness are not always found in books or in school. They are written into the inner consciousness of everyone who intensely searches for perfection in creative achievement and are understood. The level of Tenth Dan in my opinion should be reserved for men or women who reach the mental level of that degree not because they are the founders of their own systems (some limit must be set, such as time in the martial arts, knowledge, achievements, etc.) I fear too many people are becoming Tenth Dan without fulfilling the requirements.

The highest level a person can reach is Judan, and it must be kept a great honor for the very few who reach this point in life. If everyone is a Tenth Dan then the prestige is no longer there. I hope, Mark, you can understand my meaning. I am extremely upset at the present trend to promote "everybody and his brother" to Tenth Dan by other organizations who promote themselves! I can see Soke for a founder, but not Tenth Dan unless they fulfill the requirements. Successful men have learned to multiply themselves by gathering thought energy into a high potential and using it in the direction of the purpose intended. Many successful men of genius have three particular qualities in common. One, they produce a prodigious amount of work; two, they seem to never tire in their endeavors; and, three, their minds grow more brilliant as they grow older.

While many great men's lives begin at forty, their genius remains an ever flowing fountain of creative achievement until they die. They have learned to gather thought energy together to use for transforming their conceptions into material forms. While we are on the subject of genius, it may well be said that IQ is not the most important factor here. A genius may in time become a Tenth Dan, but this does not necessarily mean that a Tenth Dan is a genius.

The distinction of being a genius is usually given to those individuals who, through the use of their own facilities of intuition (i.e., "gathering thought energy into a high potential") excel in their chosen profession; however, some geniuses never realize their potentials and are never found out. Thomas Edison said, "I am merely the instrument through which a Supreme Intelligence carries on his work."

Edison realized that he was part of his idea, not just God doing it for him. He also believed the myth of the old saying that God helps him who helps himself. Success said Edison is 1 percent inspiration and 99 percent perspiration. Progress requires human effort. Awareness is important as I have stated before, and therefore I will attempt to explain my thoughts concerning awareness by making you aware of how thought processes affect the brain, mind, and body. I will begin with mental energy, or Chi, and explain as simply as possible what I think in this area.

Ki or Chi, mental energy as it is often called, what is this force? What is this energy? Perhaps it would be best for you and the students of Keichu-Do to refresh your memory with regard to some of the more basic scientific facts that surround this phenomenon. In this way it will then be possible for you to better, and more fully, understand how mental energy can act of matter and effect such incredible acts as seemingly "miraculous" cures—even at long distance—and phenomenal feats of strength. You recall the basic laws of physics, which state that sound, heat and, light are forces. So, too, is thought (a form of Ki). Thought is in part a force which scientists believe may prove to be far more powerful than any other in proportion to the amount of energy expended at any one time.

Your brain may be compared to a computer with billions of cells or information centers. Everything ever seen, felt, smelled, or heard has been computerized in your brain. You may not remember everything at will but it's there and can be used if necessary. Thoughts are the results of experiences or the beginning of experiences. A thought can create attitude, and attitude creates personality, which creates action.

How does the force of thought work? By examining the power of the brain over the body itself, we get the answer. Your brain, Mark, controls the functions of your body by means of a flow of electricity (nerves). This electricity (also a form of Ki) signals various parts of the body to react as they are required in order to fulfill various purposes. Your brain is a source of lifetime energy. When you wish to stand up, for example, the brain signals the muscles of your legs and back, which makes possible the performance of a physical act. But most of us know electricity as a source of energy, of power that reaches us from external means. After all, if you want to light a lamp in your room, you have to plug it into the wall socket to get the energy.

Now concerning this energy, Ki or electricity, you might say, "Ok, Soke Marx, but where does the electricity come from that makes our body appliances work? There is no electrical outlet into which we plug." Ah, but there is, however, a built-in source of electricity, Mark, that you use every living moment, a source that supplies more energy than all aspects of your life could possibly require. It is a kind of lifetime battery; this is God's Golden Gift to us—our brain. In the middle of your brain between the two major segments, the cerebrum and the cerebellum, there is a small organ called the thalamus. This area of the brain generates all the electrical energy that is used not only to keep your brain itself alive but also to help your body perform all its functions from the slowed down state of sleep to the most active states of participation in sports and similar activities.

The electrical supply in the body is, as I stated, far more than actually required to keep all of the body functions and your demands upon the body operating from the moment of your birth until the last breath you draw on Earth. The brain electricity slowly builds up just as the power in the generator battery system of your automobile does. But when the level of reserve that the body can use and possibly tolerate is reached and the production continues since there is no way of cutting it off, the body arranges to have the excess dissipated. Thus, Mark, just as heat dissipates, just as all energy dissipates or moves to some other time in space, so does body energy.

Brain electricity slowly discharges from the body's reservoirs. The emanation or radiation of electricity generated by the body forms an electromagnetic field of force around the physical body itself. This force field has been studied by researchers, and it has been given the names variously of human aura or etheric body or by martial artists Chi and Ki. This human aura or etheric body can be described as the radiation or emanation of electromagnetic forces generated by the body itself in the performance of healing or everyday functions.

Since the body is made up of energy, any injury to the body may mean that energy at the injured area has been displaced, by a sharp blow or an excessive amount of force in that area. Similarly, dropping a pebble in a clear brook causes the water to be pushed down, away and up, but it usually returns to normal or close to it. But the body is different in that it takes longer for the proper energy to return, thus, by placing one's hand or fingers on another's injured part and replacing the energy by using our excess, we start the healing process faster— removal of pain, etc. You see, Mark, the importance of the brain? But most importantly the mercy of God, and the Holy Spirit. Remember how many times I did that? My problem was that I never gave God the credit.

Now since the brain is our computer which is responsible for our very lives and which even regulates if it will be a happy or unhappy life, we must protect our brain and ourselves by programming positive information into it from an external view. If our bodies are healthy our brain has a better chance of success. We must be aware and in control of our emotions to the best of our abilities, <u>prayer helps</u>. Wrong, negative thought processes can and do cause our brain and vital organs to malfunction. Mark, you and I and all our students should be aware of <u>mental self-defense</u>.

For the most part one can see an attacker coming and a fist fight can be corrected by a local doctor for cuts, etc. But few people can see a mental attack and it is much more difficult for a medical staff member, be it local doctor or psychologist, to mend the wound. Everyone certainly has more mental attacks per day than physical attacks; An unkind word, gesture or even an imagined offense is painful and may create negative thoughts that in turn cause damage mentally and physically.

Over the years, one organ or system of organs after the other has been studied in man, functioning in his environment or context. It has been scientifically proven; for example that in a setting (situation) perceived by an individual as presenting a certain type of threat, that the mucous membrane lining of the stomach becomes intensely engorged, its acid secretion greatly accelerated, and its rhythmic contractions augmented. However, the stomach patterns of a man preparing to eat a meal, is quite different. Under circumstances that call for entirely different reactions of aggression or striking in anger, the individual appropriately evokes an eating pattern.

Obviously, since the eating pattern cannot resolve the situation that evoked it, it is excessively prolonged and the unused acids may cause peptic ulceration. In other studies, the large bowel has been observed in those who perceive themselves as threatened in a given way. As a result, great quantities of blood engorge the mucous membranes and motility and secretion are increased. This is the patter of ejection--one that could be used in ridding the organism of waste. Yet, when used inappropriately to help the man rid himself of an unattractive human problem (mental or emotional) that cannot be dealt with this way. Abnormal secretions and breakdown by products may then destroy the lining of the bowel, resulting in ulcerative colitis or maybe cancer or hemorrhoids at the anal area.

Studies of the mucous membranes of the nose, upper airways and lungs have shown that circumstances perceived by an individual as threatening (a mental attack) may result in engorgement of the mucous contraction of smooth muscle of the airway and even spasm of skeletal muscle. This excessive and inappropriate use may cause chronic infection, chronic obstructive disease and asthma. Alterations in the chemical makeup of the secretions within the lungs may in some cases cause tuberculosis or other problems in this area. Under circumstances that threaten an individual's fulfillment of his role as a man, the blood vessels about the head may dilate painfully (headache) and great sheets of muscle of the head and neck may go into or become a cramp.

Mark, I believe that under threatening circumstances because of inappropriate responses of the blood vessels and unusual secretions in the skin, many skin disorders arise: rash, falling hair, pimples, acne, etc. Also, the kidney may even be damaged because it may not receive enough blood and may cause a great outpouring or retention of water and salt. So also may the heart and blood vessels of the body overwork and excessively contract when an individual is faced with a crisis, mental attack or imagined attack.

When a person feels or sees his or her prestige endangered, the glands of internal secretion, the pituitary, thyroid and the adrenal glands may respond as though his very existence were in jeopardy. Thus, physical activity that is unnecessary is created and if this state of mind continues for some time the excessive use of these glands may cause physical discomfort or illness even the master organ, the brain, shares in such adverse effects. Thus, infants and children in a hostile atmosphere may not mature fully, and may grow up with a bad attitude, personality, physical defects or mental illness.

People exposed to prolonged mental or physical abuse and hatred of their fellow man, anger, guilt, or prejudice will react in various ways. For example, in prison men sometimes behave as though their theretofore actively functioning brains were severely damaged. Isolation, lack of opportunity to express themselves, repeated failure and frustration plus much inhibition and revilement by their fellows may make a person fabricate, become more suggestible, passive, or more aggressive and rationalize their own unacceptable behavior as acceptable or necessary to survive. They may abandon a value system (social norms) for one utterly incompatible with their former principles. In short, the effects of prolonged adversity of brain function may be difficult to distinguish from the results of actual destruction of the brain cells by alcohol, drugs or an accident.

Rapid and violent social change (separation from home and family, divorce), in short prolonged circumstances which are perceived as dangerous, as lonely or hopeless may drain a person of hope and of their health, but they are capable of enduring incredible burdens and taking cruel punishment if they have self-esteem, purpose and belief of faith, knowledge that they will and can survive.

The person who refuses to become irritated is indeed a rare and well balanced personality, but to get irritated and refuse to show it is the sure road to ulcers, because feelings that cannot be mastered and controlled must be expressed or they feed voraciously on the body that harbors them. Greed, fear and anger are the primary motions that stem from the instinct of self-preservation. The many other destructive emotions (mental attacks) which tend to destroy peace of mind and ultimately, health, are offshoots of these three primary emotions.

Of these, fear is the most common and deadliest. If we did not fear someone or something, there would be no reason for worry or anxiety to disturb mental tranquility and to disrupt harmonious functioning of bodily organs. There is no doubt in my mind that disharmony is the basic cause of disease, which should really be spelled *dis*-ease. (Oh well, so much for humor.) This theory is supported by many great thinkers throughout the world, one of which is Dr. Hans Selye, Director of the Institute for Experimental Medicine and Surgery at the University of Montreal. Dr.Selye feels that germs, heredity to other causes, are not the true origin of most disease, but that stress is the primary cause.

Medical researchers have concentrated on the theory that diet is a prime factor in heart disease, but stress can be the origin of this and other devastating degenerative diseases such as arthritis, diabetes, and cancer. Stress causes the body's defense mechanism to trigger what psychiatrists call flight and fight reactions, which produce drastic changes in the autonomic function of the human organism, including cessation of the digestive processes and contraction of the arteries.

When stress becomes chronic, the muscles of the arteries may no longer relax after each flight or fight reaction and permanent contraction results in hardening of the arteries. If the digestive processes are impaired, undigested food particles (particularly fatty substances) are likely to adhere to the constricted walls of the arteries, which sometimes might cause blood clots. This is why the Bible is SO important, preventive measures so to speak.

Mental defense is very important since you can see what can happen when an individual is exposed to negative or improper thoughts, stress, a feeling of being unloved, loneliness, or unkind words. Any incident that is unpleasant could, can and does cause stress. When anyone suffers from emotional stress, adrenalin is poured into the blood stream from the adrenal glands. This causes the smaller arteries to contract similar to when alcohol is consumed.

Anyway, the heart, in an effort to maintain full circulation in the force of this resistance, steps up the pulse rate and blood pressure; therefore, veins and cells in the brain may rupture, causing irreparable damage. When the adrenalin secretion causes the coronary blood vessels to contract, the heart muscles are deprived of their full blood supply and the result is pain, which is called angina pectoris. This type of adrenalin response may produce an actual permanent blocking of a coronary blood vessel or coronary occlusion. Again, Jesus Christ is; The Way, The Truth, and The Life.

Nature intends that shots of (small amounts) adrenalin to provide extra strength, and alertness (Ki) to meet whatever threat is brought on by the emotional surge. Man finds it useful in fighting encounters or sports events or in saving someone's life but continued tension, repeated emotional emergencies real or imagined as though all of life was a crisis, is more than nature intended and thus, damages physically and mentally will occur.

To elaborate further, improper thought processes can cause damage long before an actual heart attack or other physical impairment by narrowing of the arteries from fatty deposits in their lining. This process, called atherosclerosis, is that thickening of the inner arterial wall which also roughens it, and blood clots form more readily in contact with the rough surface.

Today there is evidence that emotional tension, in addition to its direct effect on the blood vessels as described above, hastens this narrowing process by interfering with the normal metabolism of fats and overloading the blood stream with the fatty substance called cholesterol, which thickens the arteries. So, I may theorize that many heart attacks are the complication of coronary atherosclerosis plus tension, and the greater the tension or the more advanced the sclerosis, the more likely the complication.

As you can see, Mark, improper (negative) thinking, bad attitudes, etc., all of which may be as a result of mental attacks, can cause not only emotional disturbance but physical damage as well. If, as I have pointed out, so many physical impairments can come about as a result of mental attacks (which go unattended), you can see why it is so important to teach our students self-defense in this area. Self-defense against mental attacks is a necessity. We experience many more mental attacks daily than physical attacks yearly.

I shall write more on this subject in my next letter. So, until then, God bless.

Remember, keep Jesus Christ first.

Soke Marx

CHAPTER 3, PART 2 - June 5, 1975

Mark,

Here is another portion of my lecture concerning mental attack, attitudes, thought processes and Keichu's Goals.

In Keichu-Ryu we strive to teach our students to be aware of mental attacks...that they exist, when and how they may come, and what techniques to use against them. This is not too different from the physical plans, except the battle is with the mind, not the fist or feet. Our students are taught that jealousy and envy are somewhat related emotions, both stemming from feelings of inferiority and insecurity, and both are a form of mental attack.

A person who feels secure in accepting love and who trusts the loved one will never feel jealous unless there is proof of betrayal. Jealousy stems from uncertainty about oneself and a feeling of unworthiness. A good relationship is one in which both parties involved are benefiting. Let's suppose that a man is having an affair with another woman and his wife knows about it. She may be hurt and decide to divorce him and terminate her relationship with him forever. She may suffer many consequences because of this decision; namely, longing for him, having to support herself, etc.

She may, on the other hand, look at herself to see if anything is lacking, to ask why he needs other women. Is there something he is not getting at home? She may then control her ego and, after talking it over with her husband and finding out some of the answers, change what she can. This goes for the husband also if the roles are reversed. "It is better to have someone you love part of the time, than not to have them at all." To share is difficult and the ego is attacked, but if real love is there, all will benefit. Envy is a more normal emotion than jealousy, but is again based on feelings of insecurity and inferiority. It would be directed against a rival, not in love, but in a field such as business or sports.

S. Henry Cho wrote an article in 'Traditional Tae-Kwon-Do' that I would like to re-write using my own style as a reference. Twenty years ago only a handful of people had heard of any kind of martial arts. Of course, today, many so called high ranking Americans claim that they have been in Karate for seventeen or twenty years but most of us who really were know better. Anyway, most students who were in had joined schools mainly out of curiosity. Later, the Martial Arts became known as an effective form of fighting and people began to join the schools for self-defense. But, let's not forget the mind. Whatever their purpose for joining a school may have been in the beginning, as they became seriously involved in their training, mental development became an important objective.

The ultimate goal of Keichu-Do as well as Tae-Kwon-Do is the maximum development of the various mental and physical potentials of the practitioner. These potentials and the basic aspects of the human being are a source of controversy among experts and laymen alike. Many people have attempted to define and identify the elements that compromise "humanness." Those that have been identified most frequently are the physical body, the intellect, the emotions, and quite often the spiritual mind. Keichu-Do and the Martial Arts provide the practitioner with a structured program that is conducive to the development of all these traits.

Through discipline in the class, serious students should expect to develop many worthwhile character traits, self-control, restraint, personal discipline, mental concentration, modesty, patience, self-confidence, self-esteem, and many others. These behaviors should be expected to carry over from inside the class to situations outside the class. However, I prefer to see God Confidence, and Christ esteem rather than the focus upon oneself.

Mark, after a number of years, these traits should become integrated into the student's personality and become part of his attitude in everyday life. For this reason, character development should be emphasized along with physical training. Keichu-Do and the Martial Arts in general, if taught correctly, are a system of physical and mental development through which the student can learn equally well to fight if necessary, to work, or to play. It is a tool for developing and maintaining good general health. Atrophy of the mind or the body can cause a corresponding decline in good health and one's sense of well being.

As you know, Mark, <u>Keichu-Do is a study which develops the mind through mental discipline and attainment of correct thought processes and attitudes</u>. It is an artistic and scientific study as well as a method of self-defense. These diverse aspects of Keichu-Do and the Martial Arts must be pointed out to the students in order for them to understand and incorporate these values. Once again, Mark, I emphasize that Martial Arts do not develop cruelty, violence, arrogance, egoism, emotional immaturity or sadism. On the contrary, the principles of Martial Arts stress the exact opposite: self-control, humility, courtesy, respect and integrity. We must all work hard as individuals to insure our development toward these goals.

True, Martial Arts emphasizes the mind and body equally. The important thing to understand here is that in finding an instructor of Martial Arts, you should look for one who has been taught himself and who teaches the mental and spiritual aspects. Anyone can learn, and even teach, just the physical side of Martial Arts, but this is not all there is, for there are at least three important main aspects: the mental, physical and spiritual.

Mark, to teach one without the other two is to teach only one-third or the way. That would be like teaching someone to sky-dive without teaching them the proper landing procedures...or high-diving off a fifty-foot diving board into deep water without the diver knowing how to swim. The same goes for physical self-defense. If one knows only how to defend against a physical attack, what will happen when one is mentally attacked? This is a hundred times more possible to happen. Ask yourself how many times you have been physically attacked in the last week or month, and then, ask yourself how many mental attacks you have had in just one day. Getting up in the morning to attend an early class or work, traffic lights when you are in a hurry, studying for an exam or breaking up with a loved one are examples of mental attacks.

Robert Hopper wrote an article about Tao – the way of nature – I agree with much of what he said. Because for centuries the study of the Martial Arts and the study of the Tao has been very much a part of oriental culture. We find records of this fact dating as far back as 3000 years before Christ. However, unlike what we so often find in this country, these two disciplines were always studied in unison; the Martial Arts to develop the body, and the Tao to develop the spirit. It is a very ancient truth that one cannot be developed without equally developing the other. In recent years we have heard great mention of the word Tao, or Taoism.

There are many books being written about the subject, and we hear it often in movies and television. Even so, few westerners really know what the "Tao" is. I have heard it variously translated as God, Spirit, Nature, etc.; but there is no direct translation of the word to my knowledge. Perhaps the closest is simply "The Way," or "The Way of Nature." However, If we use the term "Way" then it is only Jesus Christ. Tao might be the way of nature, but be it Do, or Tao. There is only one way, and that is Jesus Christ. Remember only He said "I am the Way the Truth and the Life."

The central teaching of Taoism is complete harmony with the nature order of things; a flowing with the events of nature with an attitude of non-resistance. Not a very practical idea. In this way we maintain a balance between ourselves and creation; never over-responding to a situation and never responding with too little; but seeking a balance with the forces around us. Just as yoga is a part of Hindu teaching, so the many martial arts think it important to the teaching of the Tao way. However, NOT Keichu-Do Through the correct mental study of the martial arts, like the Keichu-Do style, we develop an understanding of our physical form and our ability to expand the limits of its movement and function. Our movement becomes more natural; in harmony with our muscles and bone structure. This reduces the resistance caused by wrong or forced movement, and allows the body to come into a balance. However, if we do not give equal attention to the mind or spirit, there can never be a true balance. The mind controls the body, and if there is no harmony there, the body is limited.

From the "non-physical" standpoint, Keichu-Do is a martial art system by which one learns to do one's best for humanity by learning to value oneself as a part of a whole.

If the student wants to train effectively, he or she in turn must truly be sincere in his desire to master the spiritual dimension of the martial arts as well as physical techniques. They shall in turn be rewarded with nobility of character, a better outlook on life, peace of mind, and physical health. Keichu-Do is practiced throughout life with the true chivalrous spirit (the nobility and integrity of the medieval knight to some extent) these beneficial effects will manifest themselves. For what good is it for man to gain the whole world, but lose his soul?

There are basically three components, mental, physical, and spiritual that combine to constitute a person. In all physical disciplines, what we call "mind" must exert restrictions on the flesh. As God is to humankind a standard of morality, so is the mind to the body; it exerts the influence, which guides correct or effective behavior. When the enthusiast merely learns physical techniques such as kicking and punching he or she deprives himself of the benefits I have mentioned and merely becomes haughty because of his or her ability. Moreover, they lose the full potential of ability that can be derived by keeping the proper attitudes.

Knowing that what one is defending is right gives the student more power in the form of confidence, "right is might." We all train and study with a goal in mind, and the end result of our studying is only as good as the goal we strive for. The important thing is the mind – it is the real foundation of the martial arts. "Where there is a will, there is a way." These familiar words can be applied to better understand the philosophy of the martial arts.

In martial art philosophy, if the goal is directed toward the highest principle, there is a correct way to achieve it. It is absolutely essential that our physical training coincide with mental and spiritual dimensions. Our minds are limitless and spiritual in nature. When practitioners do not make the proper use of their minds, they are cheating themselves and others. Almost everyone will say they emphasize physical fitness in their lives. But if something is troubling them, they will postpone exercise until they have solved their problems, which may take a long time or never come. The physical body suffers. Some people think or believe that peace of mind can only be attained through religion. They try Buddhism or some other cult.

But one can get this kind of peace of mind through the study of Keichu-Do; I am not saying one does not need religion. Without God we are nothing, However it is Jesus Christ that makes the difference, NOT religion, but Christ only. Through meditation like prayer, one can develop greater concentration and awareness and learn to let the Holy Spirit control your own mind. There are many ways to learn mind control. But the Holy Bible is the best in my opinion. Keichu-Do is another, but only when taught properly.

The results are the same – an inner tranquility instead of the inner turbulence which is so devastating to physical activities. A strong mental disposition is necessary and mental and spiritual preparation are more important than foot or fist action. In our mind, we can think of anything in the world. In other words, the mind can transcend time and distance. To an extent, the body can be made to follow the inspiration of the mind through the sometimes rigorous, training of the martial arts.

Things that you formerly believed possible only in the imagination become possible in reality. Smashing cement blocks for example. From the physical standpoint also, the mind should take the lead. For example, in one's daily practice (Kata), one should always place an imaginary, opponent before himself; then, an all-out effort should be made to make every technique lethal. This method will noticeably improve your precision, power and speed. Thus, imagination plays an important role in martial arts training. When the physical prerequisites have been carried out and your mind calls upon your body to act strongly, you will find that you can accomplish many surprising things.

For example, you may remember what happened in Viet Nam when several Buddhist monks burned themselves to death with gasoline in protest of the then Diem regime. Although their bodies were engulfed in flames, they neither cried out nor moved from the lotus position. They sat quietly praying to Buddha until they were dead. You might think that this was an impossible act of willpower, but these monks were human beings like you and I. They had the same physical makeup and the same capacity to feel pain as you or I. Their mental strength and powers of concentration through study and training, discipline of their bodies and mind were the only things which differentiated them from any other person.

By practicing the martial arts, we can also train our minds and temper our bodies to be powerful enough to transcend the physical world. There are numerous other examples of great deeds performed using this kind and other kinds of mental strength, psychic healing, E.S.P., etc. The important thing to remember is that the people who perform these deeds are human like us. However, they might be occultist in nature as I used to be. In the religious sphere, deep thought and meditation lead to unity of mind and purpose with others of the same faith.

Similarly, the deep concentration required by the martial arts creates a feeling of unity with other students and practitioners. Compared to mere physical training, the martial arts are many times more effective in improving one's personality, morality, and intellect. Only by coupling the proper attitudes with much practice can we realize our goals of true and complete, total self-defense and character development.

Remember, Mark, <u>thoughts create attitude</u>, <u>attitude creates personality</u>, and <u>personality creates action</u>. For example, assume that your technique is one of the best, but your attitude is poor. If this is the case, and you are strong but without humility, there is a good chance that you will be the aggressor in an argument. When your opponent counter-attacks or offers resistance, right will be on his side. All those around you will support him. You can not defend yourself honestly and he will have the spiritual advantage.

The conclusion to be reached is that the most important part of self-defense is a humble attitude; which manifests itself in your behavior. Your pride might lead you to attempt to prove your strength to yourself or to others especially if humility is lacking. Faith in the rectitude of you own actions will also be lacking. That's all for today. I hope you enjoyed this letter. God bless.

Remember; keep Jesus Christ first, in all you do.

Soke Marx

CHAPTER 4 - January 14, 1975

Dear Mark,

As you recall, my last correspondence to you covered the areas of the mind, metal attacks and the effects. Now I would like to write about my opinions of the Ki, the super-conscious, de inhibitism and positive thought process.

I am inspired to write today on my thoughts concerning Ki (Chi) or mind power. I believe that the mind has powers or Ki that is within most everyone, just waiting to be tapped. By becoming aware of its presence on can then begin to develop this great power. Such self-mastering is a common practice in the far off exotic land of Tibet. Tibetans spend many years in solitary confinement, practicing concentration and meditation so that they will achieve the degree of self-mastering requisite to the conscious use of the power of the mind. I don't feel however that it is necessary to be a recluse and live in the mountains away from responsibilities to acquire this great power.

I believe that every human has been endowed with this powerful potential, and that this power is part of God's Divine Plan of evolution. If at least some individuals will spend the time to self-discipline themselves with self-control and concentration, becoming aware that this power is within them, they can utilize and control to some extent much more of their environment. I feel, Mark, that nothing ever happens without cause. All things are the result of natural law-positive thinking generates positive electrical forces which set in motion the law of cause and effort. Worry creates headaches, stomach upset etc. The thought waves or currents, or vibrations, call them what you will, emanating from the human brain extend far and wide.

Mark, I envision these thought waves as having unseen power which not only reaches into the minds of all persons who are in harmonious correlation to them, but, by a faculty called clairvoyance, which has access to data recorded anywhere in the world. I am also convinced that the remarkable thing called luck, which is perceived to attend the careers of most successful men is in reality not mere luck at all, but is, rather, the operation of a conscious or unconscious drawing upon the resources of some sixth sense. When misfortune, bad luck, upsets, downfalls, etc. accrue; it is due to the individual's misconduct of thought. They ceased to depend upon this greater source of power. They are out of tune with the Holy Spirit, away from the path that God made for us.

Many such individuals seem to lose their sense of intuition which caused them to draw upon this positive hidden force for their inspiration and guidance, and accordingly they become entangled in their own mental machinery and lose their high positions. They at first depended unknowingly upon their intuition, then they became obsessed by a false sense of their own importance and unduly impressed by the conviction that their success had been due to special merits of their conceited self.

Many successful people become so carried away by their own success that they forget or never become aware of intuitive faith which inspired them from the beginning. The Holy Spirit. It is true that such a person may continue to enjoy the fruits of success for some time, but sooner or later he is bound to encounter a series of misfortunes because this thinking process will not be in tune with the way of Jesus Christ, Mark, if you have learned to become truly wise, if you have learned to understand the power that is within you, you will not make this mistake. You should know that the profound attitudes of humility and thankfulness are the very emotional qualities that keep your spirits up and provide the balance so essential to a normal of above average influx of the energy, which vitalizes your mind and body.

Lord Bertrand Russell said, "Knowledge can't be locked up, it is cosmic and wide open to every thinker." Knowledge is possible for anyone at least to some degree and the Lord grants it to him who seeks. Many successful ideas seem to just pop out of the air into the minds of the individuals. Mr. G.C. Suite, as director of the research for General Electric Company, often related how members of his research group have had profitable ideas simply "pop into their minds" from out of thin air.

One idea came in solving a solution to a problem while one member was shaving. My son, you might ask, where do these ideas come from? Have they been there all the time, just waiting to be tapped? I don't really know but I think as the brain is stimulated in certain ways the mind appears to come out with the sent, if the idea God truth be known. How can this information be tapped? Well, Mark, various philosophies (this is a good example of uniformed intellectualism, I should know, I used to think this way) approach the subject in different ways.

For example, theosophy and other mystical cults believe that a universal mind is a source of all inspired knowledge. Spiritualism would have us believe that the spirit world is a source intuitive cognition. And many parapsychologists assume that there is an unseen world from which man's sixth sense acquires the strange powers and supernormal intelligence that are manifested in extrasensory perception. Some parapsychologists believe that the world in which we live is only a shadow of true reality. Others believe that there is a vast cosmic sea of memory available to the mind of man through his sixth sense. Science cannot help us say for sure which of these is the true source of the phenomena of God's gift to man. But enough is know about the way of Christianity in which the super sense operates to establish a formula for its successful use, The Holy Bible. Others, like Walter M. Germain in his book, <u>Secrets of Your Superconscious,</u> explain a four-step formula for success.

1. You must know exactly what you want.
2. You must want it sincerely.
3. You must firmly believe that you will get it.
4. You must exert every possible effort to obtain it.

This is where problems appear for non-believers; they lie, cheat, steal or kill to obtain it. I might add here, Mark, that a fifth step would be that whatever one wants be reasonable and lawful. Now, Mark, let's examine the components of the four elements of this formula.

I. **Purpose**: As a rule, people rarely know exactly what they want most out of life. This is because most of them want too many things at once and at the same time. They should, however, be concentrating their entire attention on a single objective, serving Christ Jesus. So the first aspect of the success formula is to know precisely, definitely and positively what you want. This formula while helpful in success is also the way to develop the mental levels needed to succeed in life. While not the exact way Mr. Germain saw it this is my perspective for the method.

II. Desire: Success or stepping up the mental level ladder cannot be measured by a single achievement. There are many steps in the long ladder of human endeavor which everyone must climb in order to reach the top, the pinnacle of a real successful life mentally, spiritually and physically. Material things, Mark, are merely energy converted into matter. The method of attracting this energy is to stimulate the thought energy of process of your brain into positive thought waves. I believe, Mark, that thought waves are the means by which thought energy is transformed into a thought form (like Ki-Chi-healing), in other words, the effect. Desire is the motivating force, which transforms thought forms into mystic material things

III. <u>Faith</u>: Is a very controversial subject for many believers and for non-believers as well. Many things are possible for those who really believe. The kind of faith needed to make this phenomenon work is not merely objective belief; it is a deep, abiding faith which Christ meant when he proclaimed, "He that believeth in me, the works that I do shall he do also, and greater works than these he shall do." It is the kind of faith that induces seemingly miraculous cures by setting into action a change of molecular activities, which, by increasing the vibration of some atoms and reducing that of others, so alters the structure of all the cells that they conform to the effected desire. Such a faith leaves no room for the slightest doubt about the outcome. If the mental level is high enough, then the effect desired will happen. If not, then the person being healed may be at fault, or the person doing the healing may be too weak at that moment in time and space. This is the reason behind failure - not that it doesn't work, but that certain elements needed for success were not available at the particular time. As you send out thought waves (the cause) so the condition or the thing (effect) must follow. There is sometimes a time lag and this time lag can be so long that you may not recognize the sequence. However, as one becomes more expert in this art, results will be attained with greater speed.

IV. <u>Perseverance</u>: Keep practicing; never lose faith or give up. Only those who do not really want to or believe they can't, fail to do so. Anyone is capable of healing if his or her mental level is high enough. I have since learned that God willing is the most important level (Updated NOV 2003).

One concept of Ki or Chi

There are many different concepts concerning the meaning of Ki. In fact there are so many different ideas and conceptions about Ki, that it could be compared to religions and concepts of God. With most of the translations being similar, this writer compiled a majority and will add his concept of one. Ki could be described as a form of energy. An analogy could be that humans are like light bulbs and like the light bulb whose function is to give light but cannot unless the electricity reaches it, humans cannot function without their kind of electricity, energy or life source. As electricity comes from a certain source, let us say a power plant or generator, man's life source, which we call Ki or Chi, must come from some central source of power. The power needed to break blocks, tiles, etc. Or throw someone using a Martial Art technique all must use some form of extra energy source. A small woman picking up the side of a full size automobile to free her son, this is a phenomenon which Martial Artists explain as Ki, but where does this super power and energy come from?

Let us assume for any reason you desire, that this power or Ki is a form of energy. What makes energies? Where does the energy come from? Some cosmic power or Divine Deity? This power or energy comes from something, so let us give the source a name. We could call it Universe, Cosmic Energy, Glob, Nature, or to use a term many humans refer to, God. In using a word like God, it is important for the reader to know that "God" defined here, is every particle, every atom that makes up the Universe, including air, light, water, land, living things and beings, It is important that you think of God the way you feel God, the way you have come to know God comes to some of us as a tugging feeling. It could be that everyone feels God in a different way.

At any rate there are a great many human beings who have a religious viewpoint of or about God. Let us say here, our definition or view of God is that of a Monotheistic nature. The God of Judeo-Christian, Islam's Allah, Hinduism's Ishwara, the Kami's of the Shintoists are all fundamentally different. Yet they are like fruit from the same seed. The goals are basically the same; just the methods of attaining the goals are different. Now some of your readers might be turned off by the words religion and God, but do not be. You practice some for of religion yourself whether you know it or not.

All right, now that we have the God situation at least partly cleared up, let's get to the point of Ki. If as we said, Ki is energy, super charged, cosmic or otherwise, Ki must have a starting point or source, right? And we concluded that in this sense, God is this source. Now then, how do we humans receive this Ki from God? Remember the word God to you does not have to be a Religious God that is up to you but as a Christian using the word God here as the name of Ki's source. If we stay with our first analogy, the light bulb and electricity, I feel we might be able to shine some light on the subject (if you will pardon the pun). Man, like the light bulb, serves his function by being a recipient of the electricity and while functioning serves as a tool of enlightenment, (Christ is the light) bringing a service to others. After a time as the bulb burns out, man himself burns out or dies, sometimes accidents happen and the bulbs are broken, possibly by dropping, or overload of electricity, man also has these problems.

But the important thing here is the fact that electricity or Ki is the remaining factor. As one does physical exercise—running, push-ups, weight lifting, etc., to build their bodies for toned muscles, big muscles or whatever to develop Ki, one must also do some form of exercise, but mental and spiritual exercises are necessary fro this part of development. Now we are getting to the nitty-gritty of our subject, that being Ki.

Development of Ki consists of some physical exercises, but mostly non-physical activities are necessary. As in many breaking demonstrations, while a certain amount of physical power is necessary to break an object, most individuals have that ability without prior Karate training, the most important thing in breaking is the mind over matter attitude, the feeling or (knowledge if done before) of I can do it. This is a form of Ki, another word could be Faith. Your instructor says you can do it, you trust him or her so with all the courage you can muster up, and you slam your techniques into the object. But where does it come from? And what is Ki? This might be the best approach that being to define Ki first, then find where it comes from.

Let us call Ki a form or certain amount of energy. We have already decided to call the source of Ki – God and from our definition of God; energy plays a big part so for our own reasons let us say Ki is a <u>certain amount of energy</u>. Now the next question is how do we receive this energy from its source, God? What is our plug-in, or electrical cord? Let us use terms that many people recognize, such as meditation or prayer to describe how we might receive our Ki, Chi, energy, etc. Both of these terms indicate some kind of mental or thinking exercise or petition an <u>asking</u> for sort of <u>doing</u>. I hope you understand my meaning here, as it is difficult to put into words.

Now we have concluded or at least arrived at a reasonable sound definition of Ki and its source, so let us explore further into the realms of uncertainty concerning the use and purpose of Ki. We have said Ki can be used for breaking blocks, etc., performing great feats of strength. Now let us venture into the deeper aspects of Ki as a source of overcoming anger, emotional distress, sickness, or having good inspirations and enlightenment. Not many individuals have given these phases of Ki much thought, but could it not be possible? Assuming that it is, let us now go on with an in-depth investigation.

Did you ever hear the expression; he was tired but received a second wind? Well, could that be an extra amount of Ki flowing through his body? Sure, I think so. Ki is energy. Energy according to Webster's New World Dictionary is defined as a force of expression, or potential forces; capacity for action or effective power. In physics the capacity for doing work and overcoming resistance. It is interesting to know just what the human body is made of. I challenge you readers to find out for your own enlightenment. I promise you it will be very worthwhile. While I will not indulge this information, I will clue you in on the fact that we consist of a lot of energy. Now if the human body is partly made up of energy, it stands to reason that a new amount of energy from another source directed into the body in the right proportions could repair or strengthen the recipient. An overload, electrical shock, lightning bolt, etc., can kill, but what about medical treatment for some heart attack victims or mental patients, laser operations. All have energy.

I hope at this point, dear reader, you are getting the meaning of my idea. I feel encouraged at this point because if you are still reading this far, you must have an open mind which is a good sign of intellectual behavior. You may not be in complete agreement, but at least you are thinking, and that is good.

Now, if my last paragraph is true, we can agree that Ki is our source of life and if so, could not a lack of Ki cause an injury? And an abundance of Ki heals an injury? Anything is possible; agreed? So we understand Ki to be a source of energy. Now as to how we receive Ki. We must be at a certain mental attitude or level so our mind or brain waves act as a magnet and pulls the needed amount of Ki from Almighty God that is all around us. While we all pull Ki unconsciously, think how much more we can pull if we are conscious of its being, and even more so if we know how to (let us say) our powers of the Holy Spirit to pull to use the Ki needed. Like a service station, if we know the location we can fill our needs as needed; right? Say, dear readers, you are getting more intelligent with every second.

Here I would like to say God is our service station (no disrespect), as God is the source of all sources, so what we must learn is how to get from God our Ki. Using prayer form, with the right state of mind, we plug in to the wave link and there it is, Ki. We could stop here, but I feel further definition is needed to explain the mind form of level needed before Ki can enter. Like the wave links or frequency needed to tune a radio to a certain station, the mind must fill this requirement. One must purify (so to speak) his or her mind; take out the animosities, hatred, envy, greed, jealousy, worry, anxieties, etc. These thoughts or conditions only cause static or jamming of the brainwaves, thus preventing any clear reception. An important factor, therefore, is to learn how to keep the mind at a certain mental level of competency. A clear mind free from distractions is more receptive to proper thoughts and positive ideas or thinking. Ki could be compared to the Christian belief or version of the Holy Spirit.

When one is filled with Ki, one function at top level, competent in handling misfortunes, illness, emotional stress etc., as well as creative expressions. Perfection of self through Christ Jesus and Christianity, and no other religion is only accomplished when we reach a mental level or state of mind that has Perfect Liberty. When we are liberated from our hang-ups, egos, then we are in tune with God's plan, or One with the Universe, as some say. Whatever philosophy, Martial Arts style, or system, one chooses to follow or lead, he must first have Perfect Liberty.

Also, when one finds the path or WAY (Christ) to this mental level of Perfect Liberation, his Ki should be present in astronomical proportions, and the liberated individual can be in a position to receive and administer Ki at will. Psychic powers, clairvoyance, parapsychology, Yoga, Transcendental Meditation, all have a common goal, I think, to reach this mind level of Perfect Liberty. However it is impossible without Jesus Christ and the Holy Spirit.

So now we can conclude at least at this point that Ki can be received whenever we want if we have the right state of mind and that state or level is when we have reached the point or at least close to Perfect Liberty. The closer we get the more Ki we have. In conclusion, I hope that this definition of Ki has been helpful and enlightening to you the reader, if you do not completely agree that is all right. You might have at least gotten some interesting data to add to your own perception of Ki. If so, then you had to use your mind and think, which is one purpose of this writing. Before closing,

I would like to point out that while there are many ways of achieving this goal (receiving Ki) the use of prayer has proven very successful to millions of individuals seeking truth, enlightenment and the Power of Real Ki, That which is Jesus Christ; the Way the Truth and the Life. He and he alone is the Light.

Mark, I'll write more on the subject of Deinhibitation Repression and depression in my next letter. God bless you, my son.

Soke Marx

CHAPTER 5 - OCTOBER 11, 1975

Dear Mark,

After writing you my opinions on Ki and the other areas covered in my last letter to you, I feel it is appropriate to write now about assertive behavior, repression, depression, and the physical effects they have on the physical body.

There are few people whose thinking and behavior patterns are such that improving them is unnecessary. Undoubtedly, some of your behavior and thought patterns could be changed to your advantage. I know that some of mine could. Emotions, conditioned reflexes, and your childhood training may result in these patterns.

Some of the matters I will discuss in this chapter may not apply to you, Mark, but almost certainly you will find others that do. Thought and behavior patterns can be changed if you will follow the techniques given later in this letter.

First of all, are you a negative thinker? In general, a well adjusted person tends to think in a positive way. He or she will have a reasonably correct view of himself. This person will also realize their lack of some abilities, but will direct his efforts into channels where their talents can be used. The abilities they lack do not bother these people, and they disregard them. These people are optimists; they establish goals, and believe they can reach them. They usually do. With positive thinking their subconscious mind leads them to perform and behave so that they do the things necessary to succeed reasonably well and to enjoy good health. They tend to be happy and enjoy life most of the time. And when things do go wrong, it does not upset them too much. Their neurotic symptoms will be few.

Negative thinking has the opposite effect, Mark. The end result is unhappiness, worry, anxiety, frustration, and hostility. Conflicts produce these emotions (mental attacks), and the negative thinker is more subject to emotional illness. A number of books have been written about the value of positive thinking. Since these books deal with this subject, I will not expound on it myself, but will recommend that you read one for yourself.

The real secret in thinking positively is belief. It is not easy to change the habit of negative thinking, but it can, and <u>must</u> be accomplished. No one can think positively at all times, but it can be developed into a habit so that it is done most of the time. Determination and patience are needed, with much practice on whatever techniques your Sensei, Sifu, or instructor teaches you. These techniques like the Kata take time to learn, but "practice makes perfect." But only if the technique is refined. Mark, positive habits of thinking will be of great help in changing bad character traits, in helping you find happiness, and in relieving illness. In the matter of illness, every physician knows the mental attitude of a patient is vitally important in the treating of an illness, or in the recovery from an accident or operation.

Negativism is a conditioned reflex. Our fear-based emotions spring from past conditioning and negative thinking is a large factor in producing these fears. These emotions are fear itself, anxiety, frustration, hostility, and guilt, with nervous tension accompanying them.

Fear itself is consciously recognized. We know we are afraid of some definite object or situation. Fear of death is one rather common fear. Even religious people who believe in a future life may have strong fears of death. Possibly this comes from the fact that some religions stress the idea of hell-fire and brimstone too strongly in an effort to frighten people into being good. In Keichu we want to "de-inhibit" people with this kind of problem.

Another common and quite natural fear is that concerning financial security. This is a constant mental attack for many people. Lack of financial security promotes continual fear or apprehension. Insecurity, Mark, is not only a result of lack of money, but may involve personal relationships. One of our strongest unconscious drives is to be loved. If we are rejected frequently as we mature, this need becomes stronger, and could become a neurotic symptom. With negative thinking, we expect to be rejected. One may become so afraid of being rejected that an inability to love develops, and love cannot be accepted because rejection is thought sure to follow. I have been there, and done that.

Anxiety is a form of fear, sometimes a general feeling of something unpleasant about to happen. An anxious individual usually is unable to tell why he feels this way. The fears behind the anxiety are so great that panic attacks may occur in the form of sharp and painful physical discomforts. We in Keichu strive to overcome this problem with corrective thinking. Reading good books about knowing oneself is also helpful and required in Keichu-Do. God knows how I have fought with this problem for twenty-four years. However, God taught me this is a blessing, not a curse.

Anger and hostility are related to anxiety. They are entirely normal emotions when they do not become too strong or too prolonged. Then they become a mental attack that has caused damage, and the degree of damage is determined by the severity of the anger and how long one stayed angry. You would not be a human being (even animals get angry) if at times you did not become angry, and if you never developed feelings of hostility towards others, or towards fate, or even toward yourself. Naturally, these emotions must be controlled.

In Keichu, Mark, you learn that you should not strike out when angry, or you might be in trouble. If you must strike, do so in a controlled manner, knowing well that you are fully responsible for whatever happens afterward. The Bible teaches; be angry, but sin not. Its not the anger that's bad, it's the anger thereafter.

Many people regard anger as "bad" and may have strong feelings of guilt when they become angry. Guilt may call subconsciously for self-punishment. Such an emotion may then be stifled and suppressed the moment it is stimulated because it is felt to be "wrong" to have it. This is not good at all, and can cause problems later. Another reason for suppression is fear of loss of control in anger, and the possible results if not controlled.

The combination of guilt and suppression can bring unpleasant consequences such as migraine headaches, and other painful symptoms. When anger and hostility are viewed as normal emotional responses to stimuli, they do not need suppression (At least that is how I feel at this time. I may find cause to change my mind at a later date if I find a better way.) Bottling them up does not discharge the emotions, they are still there, and persist under the surface in the subconscious.

Mark, another way of discharging or defending one's self of such attacks is through physical exercise. In many sports the player is working off his latent hostilities without realizing it. He may feel very good afterwards. Any form of exercise—chopping wood, calisthenics, punching and kicking a heavy bag, doing your Kata with all your power, even punching and screaming into a pillow will serve to discharge latent hostility. The baseball fan is working off his hostilities when he shouts, "kill the umpire," or badgers some player.

A psychological principle states that a stronger emotion will always nullify a weaker one. Strong anger may overcome fear and the angered person may attack the one frightening or bullying him. If fear is greater than anger, it will prevail, and there would be avoidance instead of attack. It is not easy to summon up a stronger emotion when we are angry, but it is possible. It is easier to overcome hostility than anger. If a man is angry at his wife, and he controls it and seizes her in a loving way and kisses her, the anger will disappear. The emotions of love and desire take over. If she is also angry, her anger will also vanish, provided her anger is not too great, in which case she may knee him in the groin. Ouch!

There is another valuable technique for many situations, including when anger is stimulated. Again there must be control first. When angry or upset in any way, think to yourself, "So what? What of it? It doesn't matter." With a little practice, and acceptance of the idea involved in these phrases, the emotion dwindles away and has little or no effect. If your feelings are hurt, if you are frustrated, or in any upsetting situation, saying these phrases to yourself indicates positive thinking, and it will ease the situation. The emotions aroused run off you like water off a duck's back instead of sinking in and bothering you. Practicing this when disturbed will be of real value. Of course, if this were overdone, one might become too indifferent, but properly handled it is most effective. Be assertive!

Now let's talk about frustration, Mark. Life is full of frustrations. Beginning in infancy, we encounter these with parental prohibitions. "No, you must not do that," and other negations are heard from our earliest years. The "I want" runs headlong into the "NO! You can't" of society

The prohibitions of parents and of society are necessary, but they are frustrating, and the basis of conflict. In later life, some of our desires and needs are not fulfilled, which brings on more frustration. Of course we cannot have everything we want, but too many disappointments can bring on frustration. It is a natural emotion, and only when it is chronic is it serious. The phrases, "So what?" or "Next time," can be good ways of discharging feelings of frustrations, helping us tolerate the situations provoking frustration.

Those who have goals and accomplish them adjust well to frustrations when they fail to reach some other goal. Continued failure, however, may bring chronic frustration and its end result. Keichu-Do students know that if our primary needs in life are filled fairly adequately, frustrations are tolerated with no difficulty. We need to love and be loved; to have a good relationship with our families. We must have self-respect and see ourselves with a proper viewpoint, maintaining a good image of ourselves, and we should be aware of how others see us, not just as we see ourselves. There must be self-reliance and self-confidence so that we can be reasonably successful. We should have realistic goals toward which we work, including the personal and the financial. With accomplishments along these lines, good mental and physical health can follow.

Keichu students are taught "Guilt is a cancer of the mind." We all have faults and weaknesses, and fall short of our ideals. No one is perfect. There is something of the caveman in all of us, instincts or attitudes suppressed by society. At times we do things which we regret and which we may regard as bad. This is part of human nature. Conscience is like brakes on a car; it holds or controls us on acting out many of our desires, fortunately, or the world would be a much worse place than it is.

However, Mark, we can be entirely too conscientious. We should learn from our mistakes, our sinful doing, and wrong thinking. We should keep from repeating something our conscience says is wrong. Dwelling on the past and developing strong feelings of guilt are most harmful. Guilt and shame can take quite a toll, with self-punishment and emotional disturbance resulting. The end result of the basic fear emotions and accompanying stress is nervous tension. This may be evidenced by nervous habits such as biting the finger nails, restlessness, excessive smoking, alcoholic overdose, and a host of other symptoms.

As you know, Mark, another technique in mental self-defense as taught in Keichu-Do is being aware that worry is a most unpleasant conditioned reflex when overdone. Everyone worries at times, and it is a normal emotion in some situations, as when a loved one is seriously ill. Chronic or constant worry is abnormal. "The worry Wart" worries no matter how well things are going. If the cause for some worry is ended, he quickly finds something else to worry about. Instead of resting, he lies awake nights with his mind concentrating on worries. He might deny it, but he probably derives some pleasure and satisfaction from worrying. In this case it's masochistic, and he may be punishing himself.

What else promotes chronic worry? Identification may be a factor, and if one of the parents was a chronic worrier, this habit may develop from dramatizing oneself, as the parent, unconsciously trying to be like the parent. Many have the impression that women are much more likely to be chronic worriers than men. The object of identification is usually the mother, but it well could be the father, or any other close relative.

A student of Keichu-Do learns the basis of worry is negativism and apprehension. By being taught awareness in the dojo, the Keichu student can recognize the thoughts or symptoms of worry, thus defending themselves with techniques. I will write about these later in the chapter. You know the result of worry is tension, thus increasing the tendency to worry--a vicious cycle. The chronic worrier must exert considerable effort to overcome the habit of worrying, particularly if masochism is involved. He must break any identification by realizing he is copying someone else's behavior pattern. One technique of defense is every time he finds himself worrying, he could divert his mind to pleasant things.

Another method of breaking any habit is the method advocated by the late Knight Dunbar, who was a great authority on habits and their formation. Dunbar pointed out that trying hard to break a habit, trying to desist from it, only reinforces it, again the old demon, the law of reversed effect. He advocated visualizing the end result desired. Greatly exaggerating the habit whenever it is being evidenced helps to break it.

Carrying out this technique in the case of worry could be accomplished by thinking the very worst, and making a deliberate effort to worry. You could think to yourself, "I really must worry hard now; what I am worrying about is terrible. What is going to happen is going to be awful"! Soon the situation may become completely ridiculous and you may find yourself seeing it as humorous and laughable.

Often the chronic worrier says, "I try but I just can't stop worrying," but what he actually means is that he doesn't want to stop worrying. "I can't" always means "I don't want to". This is a good thing to remember when the thought comes into your mind. Perhaps the reason for not wanting to stop worrying is a fear of some kind, or unconscious enjoyment in what the worrier is doing.

Worry may have something to do with certain states or conditions called repression and depression. Repression, holding back or holding down a feeling or emotion, can be dangerous to one's health.

Repression:

Since the repressed continues to exist in the unconscious and develops derivatives, repression is never performed once and for all but requires a constant expenditure of energy to maintain the repression, while the repressed constantly tries to find an outlet.

This expenditure may be observed in clinical phenomena, for example, in the general impoverishment of the neurotic person who consumes his energy in the performance of his repressions and who therefore does not have enough energy at his disposal for other purposes (neurotic, fatigue, always sleepy) (addiction without drugs). Do I fit in there?

Protection against Depression:

The most important type is represented by "love (lust) addicts," that is by persons in whom the affection or the confirmation they receive from external objects, (other persons) play the same role as food or drugs in the case of food or drug addicts. Although they are unable (or unwilling for fear of loss of love in return) to return love, they absolutely need an object (animal or human) by whom they feel loved. These love addicts constitute a high percentage of the hypersexual personalities and are often candidates for later manic-depressive disorders. They are persons who as a result of certain infantile experiences, suffer from a sever anxiety of being abandoned.

Just as a frightened child cannot fall asleep without a protecting mother sitting at his side, this person in adult life had to be sure of a protecting or reassuring union with others. He gets through life in a perpetual greedy state. If his mental strokes are not satisfied, his self-esteem diminishes to a danger point, and he is ready to do anything to avoid this point. "I know, I was there, before I found Jesus and even after when I didn't follow his Way, or walk in His Light it wasn't until I actually learned the Truth that I was set free. Now I live a much better life not sin or pain free, but a freedom I never knew before."

Castrointestinal Tract:

A good example of an organ neurosis psychoanalytically understood as a physical result of an unconscious attitude is peptic ulcer as seen by the research work of the Chicago Psychoanalytic Institute. Persons with a chronically frustrated oral receptive demanding attitude who have repressed this attitude and often manifest very active behavior of the reaction-formation type, are unconsciously, permanently "hungry for necessary narcissistic supplies," and the word hungry in connection has to be taken literally. This permanent hunger makes them act like an actually hungry person does. The mucous membrane of the stomach begins to secrete, just as does that of a person who anticipates food. This secretion has no other, specific psychic meaning. This chronic hyper-secretion is the immediate cause for the ulcer. The ulcer is the incidental physiological consequence of a psycho-genic attitude. Negative thoughts create negative attitudes which can cause negative personalities that can cause negative actions. It may be questioned whether this etiology is valid for all cases of ulcer. It is possible that the functional changes which, in some cases, are brought about by repressed oral eroticism may be determined in other cases by purely somatic causes.

Perverts are persons with infantile instead of adult sexuality. This may be due either to an arrested development or to a regression. The fact that perversions frequently are developed as a reaction to sexual frustrations with regression to infantile sexuality, are perverts. Others who react or employ other defenses are called neurotics. Even small children have sexual desires. For example, a young woman patient was unable to say no to any man, whenever she was alone, she had to go out and find a man immediately. Apparently she had an active adult sexual life, and sex to her was like a mother's reassuring hand is for a frightened child. These people in their continuous need for supplies (good strokes) that give sexual satisfaction and heighten self-esteem simultaneously are "love (lust) addicts" unable to love actively, they passively and desperately need to be loved.

Their object relationships (opposite sex) are mixed up with features of identification and they tend to change objects frequently because no one object is able to provide the necessary satisfaction (reassurance, security, or self-esteem) for long because, there is always present the fear of losing that object at a future date. In consonance with their early fixation persons of this kind, the personality of the object is of no great importance, they need the strokes and it does not matter who provides them. It does not necessarily have to be a person, it may be a drug or alcohol, etc. Instinctual behavior of this nature may also represent a desperate attempt to discharge in a sexual way, tensions of any kind. The act is carried out not only to obtain pleasure but also to get rid of an unbearable painful tension and to be retired to a state of depression. In some sexual activities, the sexual partner serves the same purpose as the drug in addiction. "Its not love, its addiction."

I'm sorry, Mark, I let myself get carried away and started rambling. Anyway, you might find some of this interesting at least. I'll write next chapter concerning assertive behavior, in my upcoming book Spiritual Self-Defense II, So until then, God bless you.

With Christ only,

Soke Marx

CHAPTER 6 - MARCH 29, 1976

Dear Mark,

I hope you enjoyed my last letter concerning assertive behavior. This moth I am writing you about mental attack, causes of mental attack and the physical effect of mental attack on the physical body. This is probably one of my most important letters so pay particular attention to the contents. This is a chapter from my Instructor's handbook that I hope to publish someday.

Identification of Mental Problems in Prospective Students or Already Accepted Students

Many instructors teach any and everyone, without proper screening by interview, or investigation. This is an unhealthy habit that could cause grave repercussions later. While it may not seem feasible to run a police check on every student, nevertheless this is a good idea. Unfortunately, instructors are unable or unqualified to get a psychological survey of each student to ascertain their mental conditions. This is not to say instructors should not accept students with mental problems or police records – quite the contrary, these individuals may need your help more than anyone else. However, the instructor should be aware of this condition so that a special program can be taught without causing the student to overstrain.

So, too, with emotional problems, the instructor can be of special help as a counselor and base lectures according to the needs of the students. It is highly recommended that every Self-Defense instructor earn a few college credits in Psychology, Sociology, Business Administration or Journalism. Courses in

Therapeutic Recreation and Special Education are also advisable to help the Self-Defense instructor. Be a better capable counselor in the area of mental Self-Defense.

The following descriptions will aid each instructor or student in awareness concerning mental attacks and their extreme results. You should be able to identify some of these symptoms. In most cases it is advised to seek professional help for any student in need of such treatment. Don't try to be a doctor; if you recognize any of these symptoms seek advice before confronting the student.

Recognition of Mental Attacks

Mental Attack: This statement may be new and heretofore unheard of by most people throughout today's world. The terminology used here is unimportant; the meaning behind the statement is important. People should be aware of one of the most dangerous, devastating, and crippling forces in existence.

Many individuals should be familiar with the words: <u>mental</u>, which relates to the mind, and <u>attack</u>, which is to use force against someone in order to harm. Now anyone with any reasonable amount of intelligence should be able to ascertain that if we use the two terms <u>mental</u> <u>attack</u> we mean an attack directed at the mind. Any attack against the body is considered a physical attack, and such an attack is usually easier to cure, assuming it's not fatal. The victim of a physical attack can usually see the attack and may go to his physician for treatment. On the other hand, the victim of a mental attack is seldom aware that he is being attacked, and consequently does not seek medical attention. After several such encounters, depending upon the severity of the attack, the unsuspecting victim may become chronically mentally ill, and need temporary or permanent institutionalization in a mental institution.

On the other hand the victim may at worst only live a terribly unhappy life-time, plagued with depression, stress, frustration, and anxiety, all results of unrecognized mental attacks.

Perhaps, dear Mark, at this point, you are becoming aware of the necessity and importance of my writing this letter. It is my intention to inform you, in a common down-to-earth language that the everyday man, woman, and child can also understand. The average and above average individuals will be able to read and learn about how they may save themselves from a dreary and unpleasant lifestyle. This book will be free from too many long and difficult words, and free from terminology used by many authors who are trying to impress someone with big words and professional jargon. I am just plain folk, trying to help people like myself who may not have the education or money to obtain help otherwise. At the same time I hope the professional educators and intellectuals will not find this book dull but, instead, informative, interesting and helpful.

Classifying Types of Mental Attack

There are two major types of mental attacks: Suggested or Foreign. Which are situated outside one's own self--they have to do with other people; and Domestic which are inside one's own self--they are assigned motives. When someone calls you a dirty name this is a foreign mental attack, but if you think someone doesn't like you, this is a domestic or self-assigned motive.

We believe there are five minor mental attacks, or subgroups from the foreign and domestic types.

1. **Verbal** A foreign assault, someone curses, scolds or uses abusive language directed at you.
2. **Physical** Usually a foreign type assault, someone might flip you the bird, make a face or stick out their tongue in a derogatory manner. However, sometimes the result may become domestic, ulcer, etc.
3. **Visual** This can be both foreign and domestic. You may actually see something that reminds you of an unpleasant or sad past experience, or sometimes you may think you saw something, but it was not really true. This is called imagined. Which brings us to the fourth type.
4. **Imagined** Mostly domestic, a person decides that their father, mother, husband, wife, etc., doesn't love them. Whether it's true or not, the emotion is real and hurts the same as if it were true. This can be one of the most dangerous forms of mental attack.
5. **All or any Combination of the Above** A person could suffer from two, three, or all of the minor forms of mental attack at the same time.

The brain according to Dr. Wayne W. Dyer, is composed of ten billion, billion working parts (you might relate to brain cells rather than parts), which has enough storage capacity to accept ten new facts every second.

The human brain has been conservatively estimated to have the ability to store an amount of information equivalent to one hundred trillion words, and that all of us use but a tiny fraction of this storage space. It is a powerful instrument you carry around with you wherever you go, and you might choose to put it to some fantastic uses which you've never even considered, up until now. Keep that in mind as you go through the pages of this book and try to choose new ways of thinking.

It is said that you cannot have a feeling (emotion) without first having experienced a thought. A feeling is a physical reaction to a thought. If you become angry, cry, laugh, or increase your heartbeat, or any emotional reactions, you have first had a signal from your thinking center or brain. Once your thinking center is damaged, or short-circuited, from mental attacks your emotional experiences may not turn out to be favorable or pleasant. Every feeling that you have is preceded, by a thought, remember thoughts create attitudes which create personality, which create action.

Anyone who thinks negatively about something because of a mental attack by someone is setting himself up for bad times. A verbal mental attack is anything abusive in the form of sound or language. To further elaborate, let's discuss this in more detail. Suppose you hear a song via radio, TV, tape-deck or record that reminds you of an old love, boy or girl friend, spouse etc., that you are no longer with. If you are divorced, broken off or a long distance from, you may be hurt by emotions long forgotten but now brought back to memory by the song. You've heard of the expression that's our song! Or turn that song off, it reminds me of someone I want to forget. Another method of verbal mental attack can come by hearing an expression used by someone that reminds you of someone else. For example, let's use "Hi Kitten," and your ex-husband or someone you loved or may still love used to call you that nickname or use that expression; if it hurts then it is a mental attack.

The more common forms of verbal attack comes from anger, inconsideration, lack of tact, and just plain old meanness. When loved ones become angry with one another, they sometimes and often do say unkind things because they are angry. Some will say it is better to say something unkind than to strike a physical blow, but a physical attack is most often easier to heal than a mental blow that lingers on and on. The Bible has a lot to say about the two.

The following are examples of expressions said in anger. Some may be offensive to the more sensitive reader and we apologize in advance, but these are true expressions and the most commonly used. (Note: I removed all the profane examples), buzz off, punk, tramp, your stupid, you dummy, you idiot, numbskull, dumb butt, pea brain, your a bum, good for nothing, dead beat, your lazy, your irresponsible, your clumsy, shut up, shut your mouth, your no good, you'll never amount to anything, fat butt, fatso, skinny butt, bean pole, toothpick, dago, nerd, you jerk, your immature, lousy, sloppy, sissy, coward, weenie, you turkey, weirdo, you freak, fink, bird brain, etc.

These expressions are all forms of verbal mental attack, and we are sure you readers have heard many more from one source or another. But remember now that you know what they are, you don't have to accept them. You have a choice, you can decide to make a positive or negative decision. The choice is yours and yours alone. Eleanor Roosevelt once said, "the only way someone can insult you is for you to accept the insult." If you get your feelings hurt from a verbal mental attack, the truth is you choose to be hurt. Feelings are not just emotions that happen to you. Feelings are reactions you choose to have. Did you know that you are in charge of your own emotions? Well, you are and you don't have to choose self-defeating reactions. All you have to do is understand that you feel what you choose to feel. This is the right path to true personal freedom and Perfect Liberty. Realizing this will greatly aid you in your endeavor to serve Jesus Christ.

The truth is that you have the power to think whatever you choose to allow into your head. If a thought comes to you, you can choose to leave it or make it go away. You have control of your mental world. Now, if you control your thoughts and your feelings come from your thoughts, then you are capable of controlling your own feelings. And, dear reader, you can control your feelings by working on the thoughts that precede them. Simply put, if someone verbally attacks you and you become unhappy, you make yourself unhappy, not the rude person who spoke unkindly. With this in mind, you now realize if someone calls you one of the preceding "bad names," you know it's not true so don't accept it, and there is no need to become hurt or angry.

A physical mental attack may come in the form of a gesture or any obscene mannerism which is offensive or otherwise painful, distasteful, derogatory or abusive. Examples might be, as you walk up to a group of your friends they ignore you or turn away. As you walk away you notice a couple of them smile, and make a certain gesture which you know is unflattering. You might walk into a room and those inside suddenly stop talking, or ignore you. Any form of disrespect from someone directed toward you is a mental attack. Someone might close their fist and extract their middle finger(shooting the bird). There are many gestures; a look of disgust. Snide facial expressions hurt as much as a snide remark. Think about it. Don't you remember ever seeing someone saying hello to someone else or yourself and then making a funny expression that might not have been funny to the recipient. A major type is the cold shoulder treatment where your wife refuses to talk to you, which can go on for hours or even days. It's often used as a tool in hurting someone, one is supposed to love. This method is a great handicap to communication.

These mental attacks can hurt a person a great deal, but again you must remember, you don't have to become upset. If they are such a manner, that's their problem, not yours. Let them have it. You don't have to participate. It's they that lose. Your friendship is a valuable commodity and if someone doesn't have the intelligence to realize it, that's their loss. There are many who would cherish your friendship. Sometimes a practical joker can become a physical mental attack, a person who is always slapping you on the back, glass or cup trick that spills its contents on you. Someone who always punches you on your shoulder can be a real pain, both physically and mentally. Bullies who push you around or duck you while swimming, practical jokes, while not really a dangerous form of physical attack, are usually frustrating and are for the most part a mental attack. Remember, even if these pranks are aggravating, you don't have to get angry. It's all up to you.

Now you may have some idea as to what a mental attack is and how to recognize one. So the next time you are in a hurry to go somewhere and it appears that you are catching every red light in town, or someone is driving slowly ahead of you, or a car cuts in front and almost runs you off the road, or blows their horn for you to start from the red light that just turned green, remember, its just a mental attack. Don't get excited and overheat your system.

Verbal Mental Attacks:

We have mentioned in the preceding chapter a little about verbal mental attacks, now we would like to elaborate more on that area. Please remember that a foreign assault comes from outside, usually from someone else. Your reactions today are the collected experiences of things that happened to you in the past. For example, a psychological biography starts at birth, a child's mental and physical being is determined by chromosomes. It's something like sculpting a statue from marble or clay. As the pressures of everyday living, good or bad, take shape so too does the individual's personality or self-concept develop. A child's home life plays an important role on his emotional being. Attitudes, feelings, ideas, thought patterns and many more personality characteristics start his personality in a given direction. Just as extreme weather conditions affect growth so too does psychological pressures make an impression that are lasting effects.

Remarks by parents such as "cry-baby," "knot-head," "brat", or other verbal assaults upon their children sometimes leave a mental self-impression that may lead to low self-esteem, or inferiority complex. Criticism is sometimes very damaging to a child and later on as an adult.

A person with low self-esteem may have more of a problem than he or she realizes. Many times this mental problem as a result of many verbal assaults will be subconsciously hidden or camouflaged and surface in assorted ways. People who blush easily, or rarely use eye contact when speaking, stay on relatively unimportant jobs, find it hard to ask for a raise, are mirroring these inner feelings. Many physicians believe that overeating may be a result of inferiority. Perhaps they unconsciously feel more important because they take up more space, it might give them a feeling of superiority to be bigger than some smaller people, especially concerning men.

Verbal assaults can make insecurity a problem of great concern, especially where jealousy is present. Another terrible trait is the passive, aggressive individual. This person often browbeats the children, wife, co-workers or anyone who will let him get away with it. They are always seeking the limelight, many times they appear as bullies and are sometimes belligerent, self-centered egomaniacs. In reality they are very insecure and hungry to feel important. Look for people who brag about their exploits, or people who are always bad mouthing others, as they tear down other individuals' images, they feel their own images rise. Downgrading others upgrades themselves. This is a false way to build self-esteem. Just think, all of this trouble just because this individual suffered from mental attacks in the verbal form.

What these victims fail to realize is that they are actually suffering from their own SELF-rejection. They have not accepted themselves or developed any form of self-esteem, and they feel like nobodies. But the inferiority feelings have been learned, and they can be unlearned, with professional help or sometimes good reading.

Verbal attacks come in many forms. Transactional analysis teaches that of the three ego states each individual has such as the Parent, Adult, and Child, which are not concepts like the Superego, Ego and Id. The Parent ego state is a huge collection of recordings in the brain of events in the past, involving real people, real times, places, decisions and feelings. These are external stimuli that are specific for every person, being the recording of that set of data received or experienced earlier by the individual. For example, if a child's parents were hostile and constantly fighting or arguing with each other, this scene was recorded in the child's Parent ego state with terror.

In this state are recorded all the rules and laws that the child heard from his parents, relatives and anyone else he comes into contact with. They range all the way from the earliest parental communications and all the rest throughout early childhood, adolescence and into adulthood. The significant point I am attempting to make is that whether these rules, laws or statements are good or bad, they are recorded as truth from the source of all security (after all adults are always right, especially Mom or Dad). These past events may become permanent recordings a person cannot erase. It is available for replay throughout life.

This replay is a powerful influence throughout life. These examples of coercing, forcing or in case of verbal abuse such as names called by others like dumb butt or lazy bum, etc., are rigidly internalized as a voluminous set of data which could hurt the individual's self-esteem and self-confidence in later years, especially if the individual acts on this advice from the past. Can you imagine someone who was told by his or her parents that they were no good and would never amount to anything, and believing this they were no good and would never amount to anything, and believing this they could never keep jobs because of their being convinced that their parents were right.

Your self-esteem and emotional competency are very important to combat mental attacks. For the best performance you need the "I can" attitude rather than the "I can't" philosophy. Your self-concept (which means your opinion of yourself) is your selector of experience. If you believe that you can do only certain types of work or other things such as sports, society may take you at your own rating and evaluate you in the same way. Then if you realize this shortcoming society has elected you, on your own recognition, you feel that since society has labeled you a misfit you now have reinforced information to confirm your thoughts about yourself.

In conclusion, let us say in defense of parents that few mothers and fathers are authorities on child-raising and child psychology. As parents, we will make mistakes. It would be nice if every married couple would by law or choice, be able to attend classes concerning the proper way to raise children, but even at that, there are many factors to consider and no guarantees that they would become better parents. Indeed, child psychologists sometimes have children who are badly spoiled. Sometimes it is easy to tell someone else what to do, but hard to do it yourself.

Careless remarks made by parents to their children can at times be picked up by the subconscious and will become fixed ideas which later are carried out like post hypnotic suggestions. They are more likely to become fixed in the child's mind if the child is under an emotional setting, perhaps when being punished or yelled at (My mom says she was too hard on me as a child, I don't remember ever being whipped by her, now as for Dad, Oh boy.).

Telling a punished child, "you're a bad boy," may sound trivial. Heard again and again, year after year, he may accept the idea and compulsively be bad. The child while probably having been a naughty boy is, nevertheless, not a bad boy. Bad, means evil. Many adults often use similar statements when scolding a child who may have been pounded into the youngster's subconscious. "You're worthless." "You'll never amount to anything." "You never do as you're told." You rebel, troublemaker, or "you're stupid." These things are common, and the results are often hardships and unhappiness for the victim in adulthood. I know this to be true, I am that kind of Father. But God isn't finished changing me yet. My mouth hurts more people than my fist.

So now you are aware of verbal mental attacks; what they are, where they come from, and a little about what to do concerning them. It is not my purpose to write a "how to" book or to advise self- therapy. If, after reading my book, you feel you can handle your problems better, great! If not, we recommend seeing a professional. At least you may be able to better understand your problem and a professional may be in a better position to help you help yourself. Keep on reading. There's more to come.

Physical Mental Attacks

The physical mental attack might be considered more dangerous to the physical body since the thought patterns create damage to the body. While the usual assaults may be common derogatory gestures such as someone flipping you the bird, making an ugly face or sticking their tongue out at you, these could be considered in another category such as in the visual area. To be more specific, we shall investigate the more serious possibilities and consequences; concerning what happens when the emotional system is attacked by negative thoughts, which create havoc with the physical body.

The body responds to emotional turbulence. Pent up emotions can upset digestion and throw so much acid into the intestine that ulcers form. For example, if a person worries too much about his job or jealousy that turns into anger or hostility, this incubation may cause an ulcer. Constipation is another form or result of mental attack which may result in withholding the bowels. The action or lack of action causes a tightening of hemorrhoids. Tension over other emotional matters also is evidenced when we see tightening of the rectum. This condition often becomes aggravated following a period of great stress or emotional upset. Surgery may become necessary to overcome the problem or at least the symptom.

Our emotional troubles (results of mental attacks) are often reflected by disorders in the digestive tract, including peptic ulcers, nausea, diarrhea, colitis, gastritis, and even tooth decay. Improper thought processes such as worry, jealousy, guilt, lust, and greed, may cause stress, anxiety, and frustration, which in turn may cause physical discomfort. Many skin conditions arise from emotional, psychological causes. Arthritis is another example. There seems to be something of a character pattern or, in police lingo (mothus aripiti), M.O. with this disease.

Like migraine victims, arthritics tend to be hostile, resentful and aggressive, but they bottle up these emotions. Their personality is often rigid and inflexible and perhaps this is a psychologically reflected in the rigidity of the joints. There can be a fear that an uncontrolled temper may get them into trouble. Conflict develops over the desire to hit out at fate, or at particular individuals, a boss, your wife or husband, an in-law, or authoritative figure, mixed with fear of the result of doing so.

This author believes that the cells of the human body are atomic in structure, and that they must maintain a certain balance of molecular activity, as well as adequate chemical elements (hormones) for the organism to be healthy. Furthermore, I agree with what many endocrinologists believe, and that is the endocrine gland system which is controlled by the mind or instinctive, emotional part of the human brain, regulates molecular activity. We believe that if the mind accepts an idea, suggestion or statement ('you're no good"). Or you suspect someone of wrongdoing, you hate someone, any negative ideas, as true as it sets in action, through the electrical force generated by the stimulation of strong emotion, a chain of molecular activities that so alter the structure of bodily cells that conform to the idea, whether it is one of good or bad, sickness or health.

So you see, if the emotions control the secretions, and the quality of the secretions determines the chemical changes, which constitute all other cellular growth. It is possible and logical that cheerful, happy (positive) emotions are like sunshine. They stand for health and harmony. On the other side of the coin, fear, worry, hate, and all forms of unkindness evolve a toxin, which tends to clog circulation, disturb digestion, congest the secretions and stupefy the senses, and it tends to destroy life. This is the very same thing that God teaches in his Holy Bible. It's right there in the book of Matthew chapter six, verses 25-27 and verse 34.

We also believe that greed, fear, and anger are the primary emotions that stem from the instinct of self-preservation and that the many other destructive emotions, which tend to destroy peace of mind and ultimately health, are offshoots of these three primary emotions. Of these, fear is believed to be the most common and deadliest. (in the Bible read: 2 Timothy chapter 1 verse 7) If we didn't fear someone or something there would be little reason for worry or anxiety to disturb mental tranquility and disrupt harmonious functioning of bodily organs. We believe that mental attacks cause disharmony and that disharmony is a root of disease. Medical researchers have concentrated on the theory diet is a prime factor in heart disease, the nation's number one killer. We agree in part; however, mental stress brought on by mental attacks can be the origin of anxiety and other devastating degenerative diseases such as mentioned before--arthritis, diabetes and cancer. Dear God, even though I knew this stuff I still allowed myself to get caught up in a lot of it.

Mental attacks, some are like competition on the job. Let's use professional football for example. A certain player is getting older and a rookie player appears to be a threat for his job. This can cause anxiety or stress, the same for big business professionals especially at the executive levels. Stress causes the body's defense mechanism to trigger what some psychiatrists call flight or fight reactions, which produce drastic changes in the autonomic function of the human organism. If one does not recognize mental attacks for what they are and continues to be in a negative emotional state, stress will be present.

When stress becomes chronic, the muscles of the arteries no longer relax after each successive flight or fight or anger reaction and permanent contraction results in hardening of the arteries and as the digestive processes are then impaired, undigested food particles (especially fatty substances) are likely to adhere (stick) to the constricted walls of the arteries sometimes causing clots. No wonder I am in such terrible shape, this is true!

When an individual becomes angry and stays angry for long periods of time, stress appears and this emotion causes a reaction. The results are, adrenalin is poured into the blood stream from the adrenal glands. This causes the smaller arteries to contract. The heart, in an effort to maintain full circulation in the face of this resistance, steps up the pulse rate and blood pressure. The damage usually begins long before a heart attack, in the narrowing of the arteries by the formation of fatty deposits in their linings. The process (otherosclerosis) that thickens the inner arterial wall, and blood clots form easier that way. It may be all right to become angry once in a while, but never stay angry more than twenty minutes at a time. Realize that you are experiencing a mental attack and that the results could be deadly, or at least damaging to your well-being. God teaches its O.K. to become angry, just don't sin and don't let the sun go down on your anger, this is particularly important when you are angry with your spouse.

Visual Mental Attacks

Visual mental attacks are both foreign and domestic. The unusual thing about visual attacks is that they can start off as foreign, seeing someone you used to be married to and who you still love, and then domestic, as the hurt creates negative thought processes which in turn becomes internally painful.

The more common visual assaults are as mentioned before, someone shooting you the bird, a facial expression, or being ignored, etc., etc. How many times have I said that? All of these can and do have the same results as the verbal and physical problems. Some of the more drastic examples of visual mental attacks are as follows: a father who is separated or divorced from his wife and who has not been able to see his children for a while. One day he sees another father playing with children that remind him of his own. The hurt and loneliness are devastating. (Man, have I ever been there and done that. That's why God hates divorce.) Or while watching television he sees a child with his dad and this scene makes him long for his own child. Another example would be a new widow seeing a man that reminds her of her dear departed husband. A child whose dog was killed sees another dog that reminds him or her of their dog.

There are many examples of visual type mental attacks. Our purpose is to make you aware, by pointing out some of them. A few you will recognize right away; others you may recognize later.

While rummaging through old mementos you come across an old picture of a friend or loved one. This can bring an emotion of joy, or pleasure, but at the same time it may cause lonely feelings, sadness or some other negative emotion. An old trophy, medal, or any object that has sentimental value can bring about memories of bad times, or good times long forgotten. It is the ability to control our emotions that is so important. When we have an experience that triggers our emotions we must be aware of the conditions. And if the emotion is negative we should be aware of it and start to control the thoughts that come from it. If the negative emotion is allowed to continue, a physical response will ultimately cause some form of illness, most commonly a psychosomatic illness, like anxiety and panic attacks.

Since many of you readers may not be familiar with the conditions which physicians usually consider as psychosomatic, a number of the more common ones are listed here. To include all of them would be like printing a large part of a medical dictionary. With some such as allergy and arthritis, so little is know about them that the picture may be confusing. There may be only an organic, basis, but usually there are psychological causes, so these are included in my list. Some of the illnesses classified as psychosomatic are, in the opinion of these authors, as follows.

1.   From the respiratory system problems may occur such as allergy, sinusitis, hay fever, common cold, bronchitis, asthma, emphysema, and pulmonary tuberculosis.
2.   Problems of the skin such as eczema, urticaria, hives and many other skin conditions are sometimes classed as allergies.
3.   Digestive system problems might consist of obesity, constipation, colitis, diarrhea, peptic ulcer, vomiting, esophageal spasm, lack of appetite, hemorrhoids, and gall bladder disease.
4.   From the vascular region, high blood pressure, coronary heart disease, sudden rapid heart beat, Reynaud's disease, and Buerger's disease.
5.   Urinary problems, enuresis (bed wetting), nervous frequency, urgency and incontinence.
6.   Nervous system, endocrine problems may show up as migraine headaches, hiccups, drug addiction, alcoholism, some forms of epilepsy, possibly Parkinson's disease, multiple sclerosis, myasthenia, gravis, hyperthyroidism, diabetes mellitus, goiter and hypoglycemia.
7.   Male genital problems such as impotence, premature ejaculation, infertility (sterile).

8.   Female problems may be many menstrual disturbances, particularly dysmenarrhea (cramps), infertility, habitual abortion, frigidity, possibly leucorrhoea, trichomonas vaginitis, and dyspareunia.

Stress and tension cause negative emotions and when we have a visual mental attack our condition may cause lowered bodily resistance so that we become more susceptible to infectious diseases and in this sense it can be said that all illness may have an emotional background. When we see someone or something that reminds us of someone or something in our past or present for that matter, if this causes negative replay or feedback, we may suffer from an emotional response. Thus, all or some of the above may occur, if the condition is right, the result may be one or more illnesses. A woman may be emotionally upset about seeing her ex-husband or boyfriend if she doesn't recognize this as a visual mental attack, she may be subject to one or more of the above.

Keeping Christ first.

Soke Karl W. Marx SR. 10th Dan

CHAPTER 7, PART 1 - SEPTEMBER 14, 1977

Dear Mark,

I would like to discuss some ideas involving effort in relation to our minds and bodies, also a short subject on awareness.

I hope this letter finds you in good health and spirit. As I continue my research, I occasionally come across some good information; and, as usual, I am passing it on to you and your   students. My essays are a bit long, but I'm sure you will enjoy the contents. I will start with a quote by Dr. Dana L. Smith. It's about a most amazing individual who, while no where in Jesus Christ's league is thought to be the greatest healer of the 19th century. They didn't use his whole name, only Phil A. But, whoever he is or was, I wish I could have discovered what he was studying. (This does not explain how Christ healed, only how we as mere humans can do as Christ commands when he sends the Holy Spirit to us.)

He seemed to understand and sense the ailments and problems of people as they walked toward him, or as soon as he placed his hand on them. With this manner of physical contact, he was able to generate human energy (Note: All energy comes from God, but it is temporarily available to pagans through demonic worship. DO NOT tamper with spiritual power UNLESS it comes from Jesus Christ himself!) to match their individual wave lengths and frequencies, (I'd use their words for understanding definitions only) and to correct their ailments in a matter of minutes. The possibilities of what can be accomplished with spiritual energy, combined with some of our present medical methods, are endless. I know this may sound a little kooky and hokey, finding the best words to describe the process is difficult. The ancient wisdom of generating spiritual energy to match each person's energy frequency...as individual as the fingerprints -- each person being an individual planet within himself. Ok, so I'm exaggerating a planet. The ancient art of healing with life energies can, in my opinion, prove so beneficial to mankind (Prayer summons the most potent of all life energies; the hand of Jesus). Introduction by Dana L. Smith, M.D. Ruth Montgomery, Born to Heal, Coward, McCann and Geohegan, New York, 1973.

Mark, this is an age when churches and other spiritually oriented organizations are increasingly seeking to revive the Biblical "Laying of Hands." We hear of instantaneous cures, cures that are variously called spiritual healing, prayer healing, or faith healing. Books have been written about the healing ministry of Kathryn Kuhlman or Oral Roberts and Olga Worral. This is about another method of healing. This kind simply calls upon Gods healing touch as a large gathering, to heal this man or that woman." This is a large pill to swallow because it teaches the power of man, but I see it as all coming from God.

My theory is that it works by recharging and revitalizing the human magnetic field, or master brain, which distributes energy to all parts and functions of the body. One can lay his ear to a patient's chest, and hearing or feeling the vibrations revealing the body tensions and the location on nerve centers which are in spasm. Then, by placing the fingers on certain areas, generating the particular energy which blends with the individual's and the correction is usually effected within a matter of minutes. It is as natural as switching the radio or television dial from one wave length or channel to another, seeking the program that suits him best. I learned that I can just go to God and the Holy Spirit fills me, and that is what the brain uses.

Mark, each of us comes into this life with varying talents, which we develop to greater or lesser degrees. Just as some have tone perfect voices, and others a flair for painting, writing, cooking, or bookkeeping, many people have a strong energy current for healing that can be further developed. All that is required is that a person be strong in his own energy, as many are, while others from birth have a weak nervous system. I know this sounds blasphemous, however, open your eyes and ears, It'll make sense in the end.

Mark, those with a strong system generate enough energy current to maintain their own needs and radiate a surplus. This is the individual best fitted to heal others, and who could be taught to direct the energy through his or her hands, feeding nerves and releasing spasms, but only in those having energy frequencies complementary to each other. Otherwise, an energy short may result. I believe we must be given the gift of healing, then this other stuff becomes possible. Be careful deciding what to think of this, do not discount all, or the way it is written. It is possible by God's will to happen just as it is described. Anyway, back to the topic at hand. A body born under tension has a weak Holy Spirit, these pelvic tensions can be released shortly after birth by a person of the properly blended energy, who is able to convey the energy to the infant's controlling field. We accept without argument the influence of the moon and the tides (and many believe the moon and planets have an influence on the human mind and animals) because scientists tell us that it is true. We do not dispute the revolving planets and changing seasons in relation to the sun. We have no reason to doubt that a magnetic electrical field governs planetary action. Why, then is it so strange that a magnetic electrical field might govern human action as well? Heavy Stuff!

As you know, Mark, we are composed of innumerable atoms, and scientists report that the atom with its electrons has the same pattern as the sun and planets in a solar system. Each of us is an individual planet. A healer may follow an inner guidance, a power of powers (God, if you will). One may view the human body as an intricate machine which can function perfectly only with proper tuning, oiling, and energy. The life-force is of electrical energy, and our bodies are mechanically constructed to conduct and transmit the human energy current.

The Holy Spirit, Mark, is the distributor of energy (Ki) to all the motor points or organs of the body and calcium is normally circulated throughout our bodies in liquid form, but any time the field fails to distribute the required energy or ki to keep it liquidated, it solidifies in the weakest sections, such as joints, and at points of sluggish nerves. This is like rusting and the nerves in contact with this solidified calcium develop pain and irritation, and as the deposit builds up, the joint becomes frozen and immobile, thus arthritis!

To treat this kind of case, one sends the energy or chi to the hardened calcium areas, the deposits then begin to soften and crumble, so that they can be manipulated; and as energy increases, the waste is gradually eliminated through the kidneys and bladder. This can cause temporary discomfort, but in practically all cases, the pain from arthritic joints is relieved within minutes, and as the treatments continue, the swelling begins to subside and then to disappear. The action comes from the Power of Powers (God) through the healer to the patient. Remember, Mark, as recently as the seventeenth century, Galileo was tried by the Inquisition in Rome and forced to spend the last eight years of his life under house arrest for declaring that the earth revolves around the sun and is not, therefore, the center of the universe.

Nowadays, we smile at those who insisted that the world was flat. But, it is perhaps equally unenlightened for people of our age to regard as mere superstition the idea that we, like the tides, can be affected by the pull of the moon and the influence of the stars on our human energy fields. Or, that by listening, we can achieve inner knowing. Some healers, Mark, have their own sources of Power, like the Bible, that explains the Ancient Wisdoms of Life. By spending regular time in the word, wisdom is received.

The Bible, created by God, is available to anyone who is aware of its existence and how to receive its Holy Spirit. A protective ring of energy encircles each planet and stores within it all knowledge since time began. All thoughts and inventions are taken from the Holy Spirit, and all such information is available to anyone who has "eyes to see, and ears to hear". The theory of energy as the life-force and body activity is as old as the ages and there are many well versed in the Ancient Wisdom to whom to whom most of this is known.

As you and I both know, Mark, this world we live in is composed of gases and energy. All substance--plant, animal, and human life--results from the unlimited combination of energy frequencies acting on these gases. Every planet, animal, and human has its own individual energy frequency to establish and maintain life, growth, and development. (Think cautiously, as you read this next bit. Decide; True or False?)

I believe, Mark, at birth, the first breath of life is our direct supply, our lifeline with God. Life, itself! At any time that this energy flow is cut off from the magnetic part of the Power it came from, so long as this energy is established and flows through without obstruction, we are in tune with the Holy Spirit energy. Many believe that in the lower abdomen is the master brain, an intricate system forming the magnetic field, the grouping together of the main trunk nerves with their branches and relay systems extending throughout the entire body. This is getting gnarly now!

I learned from my research, Mark that normally the magnetic field gives the lungs the strength to pull in all of the energies. But the field then draws its personal energy frequency from the lungs to itself, for distribution throughout the body. Some of the symptoms of insufficient energy distribution are shortness of breath, nervousness, confusion, restlessness, irritability, bloat, pain, and a feeling of heaviness. Their field, which is caused by fear, anger, hatred, shock, or improper thought, processes and deficient nerve fueling.

From Ruth Montgomery's book, Born to Heal, I also learned that a child is born with a strong or weak nervous system, which is determined at conception and is the result of his parent's energies. If the mother and father are of mated frequencies, and are well and strong at the time the child is conceived, that child ordinarily has an easy birth and a strong, healthy nervous system. If the child is the result of mismatched energy currents, and the future parents are nervous, discontented, or unhealthy, the body will usually have a weak nervous system and may also have a difficult delivery. Because of this, he is the victim of low energy and nerve depletion for most of his life. But even when a child inherits a weak magnetic field, that tension can be released shortly after birth by someone with the properly blended energy, who is able to convey this energy to the infant's magnetic field so that the infant is freed from bondage and open to the universe and is thereby able to draw his normal capacity of energy from the atmosphere (This is a little hokey, but close to the truth, the atmosphere has nothing to do with this.).

Mark, who can do such a thing? I believe any individual with a strong healthy nervous system generates enough fuel or energy to maintain his own requirements and automatically radiate a strong surplus. Such a person is best equipped to help others and can be taught to direct the energy, feed nerves, and release nerve spasms or blockage of ki flow, in a person with an energy pattern with his own, but apparently there are not many people who know how to use their power. For example, many people will claim that a certain masseuse is able to massage, relax, and relieve their pain to such an extent that they may experience relief lasting for several weeks or even permanently, while others may get little or no relief from exactly the same masseuse. Those receiving benefit have blending energies and while being massaged and without realizing it, are fed their required current and nerve energy from the masseuse, who is so strong in energy that she can feed it to others.

But, Mark, if a patient has a differing nerve energy, not only she but also the masseuse may feel sapped and exhausted after a treatment. Throughout our lifetime, the nervous system is constantly influenced by the energy from all human contacts. Some radiate energy for us, while others drain it from us. Now remember folks, I'm just writing what the other two writers had to say. I don't necessarily agree with everything they say. You will have to discern for yourself what is right or wrong.

Mark, I learned that physical characteristics occur at conception and one's individuality is determined at birth, with the first breath taken representing the influence exerted by the three ruling solar suns; this trinity which is a part of the Power of Powers forms a combination of energies from each sun at different frequencies, establishing one's very life: the magnetic field. We can use this term to explain where they were coming from.

There are compatible, neutral, and negative types of energy. Compatible, or matching energies together generate revitalizing energy for magnetic fuel. Compatible human energies as a rule are of the same group: earth with earth, fire with fire, air with air, and water with water, provided the individuals are of a different birth month but matching frequency, although many variations occur because of the different planetary positions for each individual at birth. Sounds a little "new age" to me. What do you all think? I need your input. On the other hand it also sounds great. Can you see how some folks could get caught up in this belief?

Mark, negative human energies are those of different elements, such as combining earth with air, fire with water, etc. In general, their combined action causes a depletion of the magnetic field at different levels, thereby losing its drawing power on human energy taken in by the lungs. Naturally, one can understand why proper breathing in Martial Arts is so important. Neutral human energies are earth with earth, fire with fire, etc., when the individuals are of the same birth month and do not have other complementary energies. They ordinarily do not refuel one another. They blend and act as one element, or duplicate type.

Mark, with a depletion in the magnetic field, the proper amount of fuel is not taken in, the slow starvation of the nervous system continues while they are together. There are, of course, only the general principles and there are finer gradations when applied to the individual taking into consideration the rising sign and exact position of the planets at the moment of birth. There are many other facets of fueling energy patterns. From astrology (We all, hopefully, realize the bogusness of this trap.) we learn those born in Aries are under the fire sign; Taurus, earth; Gemini, air; Cancer, water; Leo, fire; Virgo, earth; Libra, air; Scorpio, water; Sagittarius, fire; Capricorn, earth; Aquarius, air; Pisces, water (there is however some truth in there).

Our nervous system through our magnetic field is influenced by every person with whom we come in contact. True in one way or another. This constantly has its effect on one's magnetic field, thereby affecting the nervous system. If one's own generation of energy is strong, these cross energies from others have little or no effect on our nerves. If we are weakened or depleted, reaction is likely.

This interaction of energy fields is greatly emphasized in the handling of a new body. In the growing child, his needed feeding of the nerves must come by radiation from his close associates (Transactional Analysis' good strokes could be another way of saying what every child and adult needs.), and is strengthened or depleted by them. Our relationship with God, Jesus Christ, the Holy Spirit are directly tied into this. Strokes are blessings. If the child's energy current blends with that of his father or mother, he will instinctively seek to be with that of his father or mother, he will instinctively seek to be with that parent as much as possible (I wish everyone felt the same way toward Christ Jesus. He is our real provider of nourishment), because he or she is soothed and nourished by them; the same goes for a husband or girl friend, close friend, etc.

When the energies are in opposition, there is nervousness and friction between parent and child. If both parents oppose his energy pattern, a problem child may develop who is delicate and high-strung, and whose nature is a mystery to his or her parents. Sometimes a child is thin, fat, nervous or irritable because of this condition. But after he starts school, he may become reasonable and energetic because he has instinctively selected playmates, who have blending energy and can act as fuel for his magnetic field ("Birds of a feather flock together"). If he fails to find such companions, he will prefer to play alone. If such a child eventually marries a person of correctly mated energy, his depleted nerves will rapidly be restored, and within a few years his personality and conduct will have been transformed (If she is a born again Christian!).

Mark, with a relaxed nervous system, his prospects of health, long-life and success are greatly enhanced; but if he marries one of an opposing energy, his magnetic field is partially depleted; starvation of the nerves occurs, and within a short time, he finds himself beset by restlessness and discontent. This is why God in his supreme wisdom said "do not be unequally yoked." Now when the natural mating current is absent, people are aware of an insatiable craving, a craving they often seek to satisfy with too much food or drink, or drug, believing it will give them energy or strength. But the beneficial results are nil. Their nerves are not being fed, by not complying with the laws of nature

Remember, Mark, the strange talent with which I, Phil, and others with the gift to rebuild the nervous system, relieve the pressures and tensions, and correct ailments by is energizing the Holy Spirit. We accomplish this by placing our fingers over nerves and nerve relay centers, automatically generating the energy or Ki complementary to that of the patient. As a generator we have the knack of increasing the intensity of the energy to make corrections, and this life energy that we transmit is said to be several times greater than the mating-energy between people. This generated energy is not the same as mechanically generated electrical current. The body is not geared to accept the latter, which the nerves will not retain and which acts as a shock to them. To rebuild nerves, to relax spasms and feed the required energy fuel, the energies of the generator must match or synchronize with those of the patient.

When one undergoes treatment by a healer, one's first sensation may be of a mild vibration at the point where the healer touches. Then the vibrations may begin shooting up or down to the area of the body that is in need. The energy is flowing through the body from the contact point, and after a few minutes, one is soothed by a mild heat penetrating every part of the body. Instead of breathing shallowly from the chest, one will discover that he is breathing deeply, as if from the pelvic region. Pain vanishes.

Some people ask, "Why doesn't everyone know about this revolutionary new method of treating physical and mental disorders?" But, Mark, the answer is that it is not a new revolutionary method. It is as old as the world. It is simply a lost art to many. The Bible records that some people in ancient days, and some in the New Testament had the understanding and wisdom of healing through the laying on of hands. It was their method of distributing human (?) energy.

Careful, as you read this next section. The power that passes through my hands resides in everyone. Only the knowledge of its application is necessary. Fear of the Lord brings understanding, then knowledge and wisdom. Not of ourselves but by God's Grace and mercy. The healer himself does nothing. God's power does the work. The healer is merely a distributor. From birth to adolescence, the body receives nerve fuel (chi) by radiation from God, but during adolescence the body's requirements change. For continued smooth functioning, the nervous system demands a greater supply of energy, plus a mating energy.

Mark, this nerve fueling takes place normally during the sex relationship with a person having properly mated energies. This is nature's method of keeping the magnetic field vital. Nature's purpose is reproduction of the race, and nerve fueling is imperative through normal sex life without insulation in order to maintain health. Unfortunately, many people after a certain point in life discontinue….

(MATURE EYES ONLY FOR THIS NEXT SECTION)

....this natural relationship, not realizing they are inviting nerve depletion and starvation, and thus ailments and abnormal function.

Mark, this is what the doctor wrote, one of the main fueling nerves in relation to the magnetic field of women is the Clitoris nerve. When this nerve is dormant it does not properly relay fuel to the magnetic field. With a partial dormancy of the field, there is insufficient distribution of the energy, and nervous tension increases. Over a period of time, symptoms may appear, revealing the malfunction of the body. Too often, these unfortunate people are called neurotics.

This dormancy in a woman also has its effects on the nervous system of the male. As he receives an insufficient amount of his required nerve fuel from the woman, his own nervous system begins to react from starvation of nerve energy. Tension, irritability, and friction may result. Women are more likely than men to be subject to a partial dormancy of the magnetic field. This dormancy can be caused by shock or injury to the clitoris often sustained during the first sex act, during a rape or very large male organ. This is usually owing to the lack of understanding of how important these nerves are to life, health, and contentment.

You know, Mark, as a rule, a woman is slower to animate than a man, but when stimulated she will automatically start generating. However, she must receive the generation in return from her partner. He should have the wisdom to generate energy to her in order to complete the revitalization of their magnetic fields. Otherwise, she, being more sensitive, will eventually cease generating to him and accept the act solely as a marital duty.

Fueling of the magnetic field may also cease as a result of opposing energies. When the wave energies are not properly blended, there follows a sense of dissatisfaction or depletion, which many people do not understand. Every parent has had to meet the cautious task of explaining sex to the growing inquisitive child. But how many parents understand the purpose behind it? Prevention of ailments through understanding is always the best remedy, and that prevention lies in teaching our children. One thing to understand, Mark, is that the effects of energy treatment may not always be permanent. The energy field must be built up to secure it. Sometimes it takes several treatments. An explanation of how some problems occur was given by Mr. Phil A. to Dr. Smith as written by Ruth Montgomery. You draw your own conclusion--I did. This is Awesome stuff.

• **MONONUCLEOSIS**: The so-called kissing disease of young people, which is thought to be infectious, is a condition resulting from emotional repression and sexual starvation at this time in life.

• **MULTIPLE SCLEROSIS**: And related neuralgic diseases are caused from prolonged seething and jealousy. Dr. Dena Smith, M.D., studied the personal history of many such cases and in every instance she found corroboration for his statements.

• **GLAUCOMA**: Because lack of energy lets the eye liquid thicken so that the normal flow is impaired. In other words, the liquid calcium thickens and can't pass through the minute passages of the eye, and the pressure from this liquid builds up and does the damage. When energy is generated to the master eye, nerves in the magnetic field (the pelvic area), the eye softens because the liquid can flow normally out of the eye. Normal treatments afford only temporary relief, however, unless the energy is built up to retain the strength and eliminate the cause.

• **CATARACTS**: As people get older and do less about keeping their energy up, they are more likely to develop cataracts. On the other hand, when they occur in infants, it usually represents a blocked energy circuit to the eye nerves. Cataracts form from the lack of energy in the eye.

• **ANEMIA**: Most medical doctors believe that the heart pumps blood throughout the entire body, and that anemia results from a deficiency of red corpuscles in the blood. Mr. A says that the artery and vein fibers have one form of energy and the corpuscles have a different polarization. This interaction is what moves the blood and pushes the corpuscles in the arteries and veins. As soon as the energy is increased in the corpuscles this action is sped up, pushing the blood over the head and eliminating the dizziness, etc., and by putting a charge of energy to the area of the relays, to the heart, spleen, and pancreas, it seems immediately to increase the number and charge of the corpuscles (which Mr. A usually calls electrons).

• **BLOOD CLOTS**: After surgery, because an insult of the surgery to the nerves is a shock to the magnetic field, which in effect lowers the energy supply to the body, and this is often manifested in the formation of blood clots in the leg veins. It is simply that the energy of the vein nerve fibers and the change of energy in the blood, and it slows down and clots. At this point one might ask if the heart doesn't pump the blood, what does it do? Well, the heart simply recharges the electrons, the corpuscles. When it doesn't have enough energy to recharge them, then anemia results from lack of the push power.

• **ARTHRITIS**: results when the magnetic field does not pull enough energy from the lungs to supply the necessary energy to keep calcium liquid in the body. If you break a bone, a shock is delivered to the field, which reverts back to the injured area, retarding the energy at that point and causing the calcium to solidify to mend the bone. This is nature's way of mending. But when the field has a general depletion of energy, the calcium solidifies in the weaker sections of the body, such as joints, etc. Children get arthritis because the field was stunted at birth or thereafter, retarding its drawing power from the lungs, which can also bring about many other childhood ailments such as rheumatic fever, asthma, croup, colic, and hypertension which follows throughout life unless it is corrected with the energies.

• **CHILDBIRTH**: They'd be a lot better off to be born the natural way as nature intended. Forceps can do irrevocable damage unless the shock can be released from the body's magnetic field soon after birth. Also, if a mother is heavily sedated before giving birth, her own field is partially dormant and she imparts this shock to the infant. It is the same with spinal anesthesia, and it is the same when a mother is in prolonged labor is so tense or afraid that this tension is automatically delivered to the feet of the newborn, and there are many other facets.

Mark, if this tension can be released from the field of the newborn, so it can draw its necessary capacity of energy from the lungs to the field, the infant is in harmony with the universe and will have a chance to grow and develop physically and mentally. The high priests of ancient days understood how to blend the energy to release these tensions and recharge the field. When the field was opened to the universe by releasing any bondage delivered to it from the parent or from a forced or difficult birth, this was the original baptism.

The question of why, some babies are born with cerebral palsy and congenital heart defects is answered, by Mr. A. "Most come from this tension of birth, which manifests itself in all the other ailments of childhood. Because such a baby lacks resistance, he is wide open to ailments and this tension remains throughout life if it isn't released, subjecting a person to a life plagued by ailments. When a pregnant woman gets angry or tense, fearful or resentful, this tension is delivered to the body's field. The mother should be relaxed and serene so that she will not tense her own field and give birth to a child who is angry and resentful.

• **CANCER**: When the tissue doesn't receive the necessary life energy, then a weaker section of the tissue begins to deteriorate, shutting itself off from energy; the tissue dies and gas forms in the cells, causing bloat and expansion. Because of low energy, the live cells don't have the resistance to slough off the dead ones, so the dead cells deteriorate the live ones. It's something like one bad apple in a barrel gradually causing all the others to rot. When this condition exists, any shock or insult to the body, further weakening it will intensify and speed up the deterioration process.

Mark, when the energy is brought up to capacity, to strengthen the live cells so that they are able to fight the dead cells, the dead cells will slough off, unless the malignancy is in the final stages. The dead cells ordinarily have a tendency to disintegrate, sometimes sloughing off like strings. Many ailments are caused because the magnetic field doesn't pull enough energy from the air breathed into the lungs to supply the different parts of the body, and that when weaker sections are not supplied their necessary energy, abnormal function results. One might ask, why, then, does one person develop a cancer and another a heart condition? This is the result of their own energy pattern.

Mark, each organ and part of the body has its own intelligence, directed from the brain. The action and reaction and interaction, plus the individuality of the person's energy frequencies, all influence the pattern of health or ill health. There are so many facets to the energy frequencies in the operation of a body that it would be impossible to cover it all here. The body is the most sophisticated of all impulse relay machinery. It combines the system similar to the telephone, computers, and other electronic devices. However, Mark, the body functions on human ray energy instead of the standard electrical energy. Standard electrical shocks the body and is not retained by it. The body will retain only human ray. Man hasn't scratched the surface of this object yet.

• **MENTAL ILLNESS**: is purely and simply tension in the magnetic field. It results from just tensions in the field, like most of the other ailments. Many mental conditions are the result of extreme tension in the field, or master brain in the pelvis, which causes the secondary pressure on the subsidiary brain in the skull.

• **SENILITY**: is the starvation of the magnetic field and is starvation of the brain. If the natural mating energies are kept up to capacity, the field can supply the necessary energy to keep the subsidiary brain alert, eliminating the slowing down of the brain as well as the body aging which occurs over the years. If the field doesn't receive its energies, this gradually results in childishness and senility.

Mark, the life force is of human ray energy, so the body must be mechanically constructed to conduct, transmit, and be activated by the human energy current. Thought control, thought direction, and discrimination are some of the many energy impulses. This individual's energy of the brain, drawn from the numerous energies in the air we breathe, supplies the subsidiary brain within the skull, and all organs of the body and relay centers--the entire human structure--making each person a unique individual mechanism. This energy action and reaction on all intelligence centers of the body is life.

Mark, you know we must respect the body as an individual "Temple of the Holy Spirit." No person should try to own another. We should assign ourselves to assist and to help one another, but never try to own or possess. Jealousy is a deadly disease, which disintegrates the body. There should be an open hand for all. Each person is free to operate his own "Temple" unbound by any strings, only to serve almighty God.

Where jealousy enters, anger follows, and anger and fear are the two deadliest enemies to our human mechanism, causing the tension which limits the energy from the lungs to the brain. What you send out, whether in thought or action may come back to you. Ego is also a deadly thing because you level yourself. Once you are full of self-satisfaction and think you have all the answers, you close yourself off from receiving wisdom from the Bible.

•   **RELIGION:** The real church is within each individual. Every person is responsible to God. The highest universal wealth is to be contented and to be at peace within yourself, in Gods will, serving Him. The more contented one is, the more relaxed, and the more the mind can then tune to the wisdom from the Holy Bible, and the power of powers (Holy Spirit). And the more wisdom one has, the easier life is, because what people understand, they do not fear.

Instinct, you are born with, education, you must acquire. Wisdom can be dampened and distorted by education. Unless we have a clear field at birth, or unless the birth shock is released, we must rely solely on education. Mr. A believes that the so-called Tidings of Ancient Times was to spend ten percent of ones time receiving wisdom from those more advanced than ourselves, and another ten percent giving their wisdom and knowledge to those with less than ourselves. Mark, we must reach for the higher and give to the lower, according to our level of wisdom. This is almost Biblical! Close enough to fool many. If everyone were doing this, Mark, people wouldn't be impairing their health by trying to outmaneuver each other on the present monetary basis, or in any other way. This would keep the human cycle closer to the natural cycles of the universe. As you sow, so shall you reap. Mark, the greatest wealth is contentment within and to maintain it we must work at it, by obeying the Word of God in the Bible.

Mark, the Holy Spirit is where we receive our power. Wisdom comes to us from the Bibles protective knowledge. Here all wisdom and knowledge are stored. There is nothing new under the sun; it's simply a matter of being in tune to receive it. Like a certain channel, on TV or a station on your radio. The waves from the Lord, Mark, come to us through our brain, are sometimes automatically translated into words, or pictures (Visions like extra sensory perception).

There is only one son of God, and he is the source, and the Holy Trinity is the Father, Son, and Holy Spirit. Wrong things lead to harnessing this great power for the destruction of mankind. Can you see how the new age folk become so messed up? God is the ONLY Power of Powers. But even the lost scientists are accepting evolution over the Bible as truth.
May God bless and keep you.

In Christ Jesus I remain.

Karl W. Marx, Sr.

CHAPTER 7, PART 2 - FEBRUARY 7, 1978

Mark, today I am compelled to write about some of my lectures here at the University. My subject is awareness. As you know, Mark, awareness is one of the keys of life and happiness is one of the major things that sets the martial artist apart from the average person. In my class today I spoke of the possibility that of the thirty students present, one or more of them might be dead within a year. A gruesome subject to be sure, but nevertheless, quite possible. But I explained that my prediction could be changed, if they the students, would become more aware of themselves and their environment. For example, a student is driving from one town to another. Coming from the other direction is a drunken driver. Without awareness, the possibility exists that the drunk driver's vehicle may swerve into the lane of oncoming traffic and hit my student's car. The students clamored, "yes, but that's fate; nothing could have prevented such an accident."

I contend that the accident might have been averted if the student had been aware of the drunken driver's being in the oncoming traffic lane. How could that happen? Psychic ability? No! A simple safety device called a CB radio (or today a cell phone) could have changed the situation. Had the student been aware of the convenience and practicality of having a CB (or cell phone) in his or her automobile, he might have heard oncoming CB equipped vehicles calling ahead by some five to ten miles, warning everyone with a CB of the hazardous driving conditions ahead; namely the drunk driver. Thus, the student could have been forewarned of the location and description of the drunken driver's car. With this information, the student would be on the alert and could pull over to the side of the road until the danger passed. Thus, awareness could alter the future. When most people see the sky as dark and cloudy, they can assume, in most cases from past experience, that rain will follow. But, a small child who knows not the danger of a snake might try to pick one up. Awareness, like experience, is an important trait. That is why reading your Bible and having a pastor to teach what it says is so important.

Awareness can help us to understand our true feelings about ourselves, and others, thus, possibly preventing unnecessary mental attacks. For example, Mark, the term <u>Love</u> is a misunderstood word and emotion. There are degrees of love like degrees of rank in martial arts or temperature. Uncontrolled love can be dangerous to the giver, and a problem for the receiver. I recently counseled an individual who had broken up with his girlfriend of fourteen months. The break-up was not a pleasant happening for either party because of my student's overreaction to it. He was hurt and very angry and acted rather immaturely and not in his best interest. He suffered mental anguish for over five weeks and almost had a complete nervous breakdown. He contends that he loves the girl and that he cannot do without her. My student has a long history of insecurity and low self-esteem. Apparently what he really had for his girl friend was a strong <u>need</u>, a need for the good strokes he so desperately lacked as a child and that she gave him as an adult.

You see, Mark, need and love are two different things, which are often confused as the same. A person can need someone but not love him or her. Loss of need causes hurt and anger. But, loss of love causes hurt for a short time, but not anger, <u>never</u> anger, at least it shouldn't. Pure love could be the ability to give up someone we love to another person, or just breaking up, without being angry at the person leaving. To wish them well and to be happy that they are happy; hard, yes, but true. When we are selfish and greedy, there is little love.

Mark, pure love might be defined as follows:

Love, real and true, pure and selfless, could be the unselfish giving of one's self, physically and emotionally, without expectations. When we accept someone totally for what and how they are, in all ways, without needing to change them, this could be a form of pure and true love.

Love is given, and in many cases earned. Does a father love his son just because he is his son? A father may say so because he may not be able to admit his real feelings. But, can one love something that is evil and a constant problem? Children should earn the love of their parents and parents should also earn the love of their children. "Blood is thicker than water" is just a group of words. Just because someone is a parent does not mean that their children should love them, especially if they are cruel and unfit parents. The Bible warns against that.

Mark, love can also be lost. People fall out of love as often, or more, as they fall into love. And, the word <u>fall</u> may have some significant meaning.

Many people will be offended by my work, but that is their problem. I do not need everyone to agree with me. Mark, a person can love someone, but not like them. Also important in a relationship is that we also like the ones we love. Your wife or girl-friend, should also be your best friend. I may love my wife, but if she were lazy and a messy house-keeper, hated to cook and was often unkind to me, I might not like her very much. At least, I would not like some of her traits. But,

I could still love her. She may be good and considerate in other ways, such as loving me, or liking to do nice things for me, encouraging me to do well in college, helping with my class teaching other students for me, etc. She may have many good qualities about her that I enjoy. So, I may put up with her shortcomings. I hope you understand my meaning. After all she would have to put up with me, and my all my shortcomings also.

Mark, so many couples break up over little insignificant things that appear astronomical to them because they are too angry and confused to know better. A man may believe he loves his wife or girl friend. One day he sees her with another man. Insecurity may creep up and before he knows what is happening, he has become suspicious and angry. Pride and ego, combined with insecurity, will cause him to become rather unrealistic. Sometimes he will break up their relationship without letting her explain. Mark, many people need strokes and get them any way they can. Right or wrong is irrelevant. Truth is what prevails.

A woman or man may love their spouse, but be unfaithful from time to time. This has nothing to do with love, it's lust. Lust is sometimes thought to be more powerful than love. A husband may be away from home more than his wife can tolerate. If she needs more strokes than average, she could have a mental breakdown or physical problems. His or her subconscious mind might overrule his or her conscious mind, push under the guilt, moral and civil codes (mores) of our society, for a short while. And Bingo! He or she becomes involved with someone else. So he/she may still really love his/her spouse but her needs are even greater. Self preservation is a very strong emotion. Satan utilizes our lustful need, along with greed, ego, pride, selfishness, inconsideration, so be mindful!

Mark, I'm not advocating adultery; I'm just explaining why it happens sometimes. If she is a good wife and mother when her husband is home, takes care of his needs, why should he divorce her and punish his children in the process? Vice-versa, of course. This goes for the woman who finds out her husband has been unfaithful.

Enjoy your mind.

Soke Marx

CHAPTER 7, PART 3 - AUGUST 4, 1978

Mark, today I am inspired to write about assertive behavior, which I believe is a most important aspect of life. For more information I suggest reading "*Your Perfect Right*" by Robert E. Alberti and Michael L. Emmons (both PhDs), especially the Foreword written by John Vasconcellos. Like Mr. Vasconcellos, I believe we are undergoing significant changes in every aspect of our society (just don't believe everything they believe. I used to and when I became a Christian I learned the truth): religion, family, work, life style, education, and government. Many of our social institutions through which people found security in the past are no longer secure or present in the same way. Education, like society and all its other institutions, is experiencing painful and profound crisis and confusion (note the date).

Mark, what we are going through now is the deepest and most dramatic of changes: how the human being views the human being (himself and others), how man envisions or sees himself as a person, what it means to be human, what consciousness means, what it means to have a body, mind, soul, to express emotions, and to relate, communicate authentically and correctly in the best interest of all. (They encourage being wise in their own eyes, we know what that brings don't we?) In traditional Western culture, man has been conditioned to see and experience himself in negative ways, with much fear (God will strike you down), shame and guilt (we are all born into this world with original sin because of Adam and Eve). Whatever the relationship, be it parent and child, teacher and student, religious leader and worshipper, politician and constituent, man was impressed to look outward and upward to the authority figure for instruction on how he ought to be. Which is how it should be. The fear of God being understanding, then knowledge and wisdom. Mr. Vasconcellos and Mr. Alberti along with Mr. Emmons missed the mark, of Christ's view.

Today, however, this relationship is radically changing. Many people are looking inward and envisioning personhood in a positive way. New Age, name it and claim it attitude.

Mark, when you and I radically change our self-concept (or a better word is self-esteem, by the secular world. It should be Christ-esteem by Christians.), then all social structures and relationships might prosper. That way is no longer adequate, Mark. Perhaps the best evidence emerges from what we are hearing throughout the country and the world. Every group concerned with education (conservatives and liberals, educators and students and parents, all races, both sexes) is telling us emphatically that reading, writing, and arithmetic have been joined by a fourth basic goal of education--self esteem. (that is a bad thing, Mark) They believe self-esteem is a basic, vital goal of every human relationship and institution. I believe too much emphasis is put on self.

The goal of Christ-esteem, and the demands of many humans, Mark, make it clear that the very questions about humanness and human nature and human potential are the most important questions for martial arts schools and education as a whole today. Mark, I personally want to see our schools--all schools, martial arts or public educational--become places where students, teachers, Sensei, Sifu, administrators, trustees, and parents together explore what it means to be human. And it is possible, as well as necessary, to involve the entire community, even its most traditional members, in a dialogue about Christ-esteem and about freedom and responsibility and honesty (authenticity) and loving (caring). Though sadly lost in our current dealings with each other, these remain very basic traditional values.

Unless we do that, Mark, in our country, or anywhere else in the world, we simply aren't going to resolve our major social problems: violence, drug abuse, racism, and war. (Love your neighbor as yourself.) Building Christ-esteem, increasing our understanding of ourselves and facilitating (helping) appropriate human behavior are becoming even more vital and inherent responsibilities of our martial art and educational system. Learning to be assertive, Mark, is education for living, and for making society more human too. Self-expression is essential to happiness and success, and man suffers if he fails to express himself. Unfortunately, cockiness or hostility, is basically spontaneous in the expression of feelings and emotions, and is generally looked up to and admired by some others. As you know, Mark, sometimes people mistake aggression for assertion, but the assertive individual does not malign others or deny their rights, running roughshod over people.

The Bible teaches not to lord over others. On the other hand, the truly assertive person is open and flexible, genuinely concerned with the rights of others, yet at the same time able to establish very well his own rights. Here is where I am in disagreement with the author of "*Your Perfect Right*".

The authors of "*Your Perfect Right*" believe the basic structures of the family, education, dojo and business worlds leads to the conclusion that assertive behavior is frequently squelched among three levels. Moreover, the basic teachings of most religious organizations have frequently inhibited complete expression in interpersonal situations. Women, children, and members of ethnic minorities in the United States have characteristically been taught that assertive behavior is the province of the white male adult. Says who? Indeed, such attitudes run deep and die hard in our culture. It has been extremely difficult for the "haves" to acknowledge the human rights of the "have nots." You know, Mark, here in America the gains resulting from the civil rights movement of the 1950's and 1960's were slow, painful and tragically costly. The Civil Rights Acts of 1964, 1965 and 1968 were helpful on freeing the people from personal inhibition, but resistance by the status quo ante set have been strong.

More recently, (back in the 80's and before.) women have encountered similar resistance to their new efforts of self-assertion. Their husbands, their employers, their legislators have all demonstrated reluctance ranging from foot-dragging to open hostility and political battles. Yet women too are making overdue gains in recognition of their individual rights. Mark, our cultural orientation to the development of appropriately assertive behavior is inadequate. We in Keichu-Do hope to in our own way remedy this. We must begin to value and reward the assertions of each individual, acknowledging his or her rights to express themselves, by honoring their right to an opinion, right or wrong, and recognizing their unique contributions.

Mark, in the family, the individual is usually promptly censored if he (or she) decides to speak up for his rights. Familiar admonitions are: "Don't you dare talk to your mother (father) that way!" "Children are to be seen, not heard." "Never let me hear you say that word again!" Obviously, these common parental commands are not conducive to a child's assertion of self. But are necessary to teach proper respect. I may have written you before concerning my feelings about this, Mark, and I apologize if I'm repeating myself, but "two times read is better than not read at all." Some teachers are guilty of anti-assertive behavior in basically the same manner as parents.

The residue of parental and educational upbringing affects our functioning in our occupations and daily lives. Every employee is aware that typically one must not do or say anything that will "rock the boat" in an organization. The boss is "above" and others are "below" and feel obliged to go along with what is <u>expected</u> of them even if they consider the expectations completely inappropriate. (However, who is authorized to determine proper work procedures than the employer? What is written in *"Your Perfect Right"* is part truth and part false teachings.) Employees' early work experiences teach that if you "speak up" you are likely not to obtain a raise or recognition (except as a troublemaker), and you may even lose your job. One learns to become a "yes-man" or "company man" to keep things running smoothly, to have few ideas of your own, to be careful how you act or what you say lest it get back to the boss.

The lesson is quite clear, in effect to be non-assertive in your work. Heck, Mark, even in our most respected organizations, the teachings of contemporary churches seem to indicate that to be assertive in life is not the "religious" thing to do. Such qualities as humility, self-denial, and self-sacrifice are usually fostered to the exclusion of standing up for oneself. There is a mistaken notion that religious ideals of brotherhood must, in some esoteric way be confident in relationships with others. This is not true, it is a lie from the pit of hell. Mark, I believe that being assertive in life is in no way incongruent with the teachings of the major religious groups. These fellows appear to be a bit liberal.

They believe that to escape from freedom-restricting inhibited behavior allows the individual to be of more service to mankind as well as to himself. So to them sin is OK? Doing your own thing, "my body is mine, I can kill my unborn or almost born baby because I have no guilt feelings." I feel, Mark, that it is not healthy for a person to suffer guilt feelings for being himself. Each person has the right to be and to express himself, and to feel good (not guilty) about doing so, as long as he does not hurt others in the process, or is not sinful and against God's Word and Will.

I will write more on this subject at a later date. I must close for now.

With Christ as the Way.

Karl W. Marx, Sr. Soke, Keichu-Do

CHAPTER 8 - AUGUST 7, 1978

Dear Mark,

Please excuse my laziness, but this month I will just send you a copy of my lecture as it is. Admittedly it covers the same information as before but with just a small difference. I hope the difference makes the difference. Pardon the pun.

Today students, I will continue my discussion concerning the seven elements commonly causing mental attack or emotional ailments. In my last lecture, I covered conflict and motivations (both forms of mental attack). Today I will discuss a few more. I will start with the effects of suggestion.

Everyone is suggestible to some extent or we would not be able to learn. Suggestibility should not be confused with gullibility. One of the most effective ways of making suggestions effective is repetition, impress in them on the subconscious. As children we may repeatedly be told something until it is unconsciously accepted and then carried out. If a child is not doing well in school and is reproached again and again by a parent with such remarks as "You are just stupid," "You can't seem to learn," such statements may be accepted and believed by the child. He may then become unable to learn easily, although he has good intelligence. Thought processes create attitude, which creates personality, which creates action.

Many people fail to realize the power and effect of suggestion. It is one of the most common causes of emotional difficulties (MENTAL ATTACKS). In Keichu, we strive to locate and remove such negative suggestions by deinhibition. A trait or symptom may be largely or entirely caused by some statement, which becomes a fixed idea in the subconscious mind. It can become a conditioned reflex and is carried out exactly as if it were a posthypnotic suggestion. The things people say can and do affect future thoughts and behaviors of those receiving the suggestions or statements. Parents, teachers, brothers and sisters, friends or enemies can hurt someone deeply and chronically by cruel statements said in anger. "You dumb cluck!," "Hey ugly!," "You'll never amount to anything," "Your crazy," "Your just like that drunkard father of yours!," "Hey stupid!," "Your weird," "Hey creep!," "You're a bum," "I hate you," "I cant stand you," "You make me sick," "You were a mistake!," etc., etc.

Lack of good strokes, attention, love and affection may cause a child to feel inferior, unloved or unwanted; thus he may develop low self-esteem and an inferiority complex; a chronic case of mental attack.

Now, students, let's cover identification. All children are imitative. "Life is like a mirror sometimes." Children frequently try to be like their parents or someone they admire. They will sometimes copy the behavior of others who are close to them. This stems normally from love for a parent. Even a not so loved parent may be imitated because he seems all-powerful; he tells the child what he can or cannot do, and he has the power to punish the child. The young one wants to be big and strong and powerful like the parents. This form of behavior is called identification. It means dramatization. The attempt to be like a parent will produce similar traits, even some illness which the parent may have.

If a mother or father is greatly overweight, the child may identify with them and become overweight. This is a frequent factor in obesity. A father with a bad temper, little patience or tolerance may have a son or daughter with the same bad habits. Children are many times the reflections of their parents. This is not to put blame on the parents, but what you plant is what you pick, or biblically what you sow, so shall you reap; along with the natural weeds that come along the way. "The better a garden is kept, the better the produce."

My next subject will be on masochism, or self-punishment. None of us wear wings and it is only human nature at times to do things that we regret and to have the wrong kind of thoughts (it is ok to feel bad about something you feel you did wrong, and you don't have to do it again, but under no circumstance should you ever feel beyond forgiveness. Guilt is a cancer of the mind and serves no purpose but to destroy. We need God's merciful forgiveness). If you make a mistake the subconscious mind may then decide that such actions or thoughts require punishment. It would even seem that the nicest people are most likely to have strong guilt feelings and then to punish themselves. Very religious people are an example (Bear in mind, religious religion is not the answer, the truth lies in a "relationship" with Jesus Christ, and not in religion). Mental hospitals are full of religious people who could not live up to the expectations they or others had set for them. They have an overgrown conscience, and punishment from God is expected by them, but it is really themselves that subconsciously punish themselves.

Dr. Karl Menninger, a very prominent psychiatrist, summed it up in his book, "Man Against Himself." Extreme self-punishment may bring actual suicide or a fatal psychosomatic illness, heart attack, ulcer, etc. Masochism is a frequent part of emotionally caused disease, and to overcome it the source of guilt should be explored. The goal then is acceptance by the subconscious that punishment is no longer necessary (However, the truly wicked shall not go unpunished). A common factor in alcoholism is unconscious self-destruction. The need to be hurt sometimes may lead a person to become accident prone, or sexual promiscuity, degradation, requesting to be whipped or spanked while, during or after intercourse. All symptoms that need to be corrected. Now students, I hope you are beginning to get a picture of how mental attacks develop and how to defend yourself against them.

My next topic will be past experiences. Past events of one kind or another are usually implicated in psychosomatic illness and other disturbances. Guilt feelings arise from past happenings, as do suggestions. Unacceptable ideas and thoughts originate in the past. Uncovering these episodes is an important part of psychotherapy and Keichu-Do. In learning to protect yourself from mental attack you should each look at yourselves to see if any of the above elements can be found in you. Then ask God for forgiveness in Jesus Christ's name and forget the past. No guilt, no illness. Only Gods riches!

Now I will write about how bad emotions can and do injure your health. When we suffer from emotional troubles, their results take widely different forms. Most of, not all of us, have developed some character traits and habits of thinking which are harmful at times, perhaps greatly so. Then can be tremendous handicaps. No one likes to think of himself as neurotic, but we all can develop neurotic symptoms of one type or another. It is a part of being human. It would be impossible for anyone to be so well adjusted and so free from psychological disturbances as never to have had a psychosomatic illness (Except Jesus). Even a cold may have emotional causes. Many accidents are unconsciously self-inflicted. Even a slip of the tongue is subconsciously motivated. In Keichu-Do, we want to help you to help yourself. With prayer treatment or Christ therapy, in most cases you will be able to defend yourself from mental attack.

The most severe mental illnesses are the psychoses. However, a neurosis may also be a severe condition, completely incapacitating a person. The conditions require treatment by a psychotherapist and self-treatment might not be advised without professional help.

Bible therapy as we may call our method of protection training is likely to be easiest and most effective in changing our mental attitudes, character traits and our wrong patterns of thinking. Emotional illnesses may result from these and correcting them may bring relief from the illness or prevent the illness in the first place. "An ounce of prevention is better than a pound of cure." Just like a physical attack, we can only teach you so much of how to defend yourself against attack, if you are hit and hurt, then it's time for professional help in the form of a psychiatrist, etc. Through Keichu, we learn that with any form of emotional disturbance, certain emotions, feelings, and ways of thinking seem to be commonplace. Anxiety, in varying amounts is almost certain to be present.

Anxiety might be defined as a feeling of apprehension or a fear, without any definitely known reason for it. Another common symptom is fatigue. Most emotionally disturbed people complain of fatigue and lack of energy. "This is not to be confused with people who work hard and long hours or study late hours for exams. They will naturally be tired." Even though sleep is normal, the person wakens in the morning feeling tired. There are really two kinds of fatigue; physical through exertion, and emotional or mental. Mental fatigue is not well understood, but is commonly thought to come from too much mental activity, and from the inability to solve our problems. One must not overreact here. Good judgment is necessary to recognize a true attack by symptoms just like one would not strike a blow to another without proper provocation.

Another symptom of mental attack is negativism. A negative attitude seems to go hand in hand with emotional and neurotic difficulties. Everything is I CAN'T instead of I CAN. I can't really mean I don't want to. There is a feeling of hopelessness and helplessness. Expectation of the worst is quite likely to bring trouble, for it is a form of negative suggestion and the subconscious may then cause behavior which will bring trouble.

Feelings of inferiority and insecurity are very common symptoms of mental attack. To some degree, such emotions are almost universal. Even the brash, cocky, self-assured individual may be showing these characteristics in an unconscious effort to cover up his real feelings of supposed inferiority. This compensation is similar to the behavior of the bully, who is actually hiding his or her cowardice, or the person who is cruel at times to others, even those whom they love very much. Cruelty is another symptom of mental attack and should be dealt with quickly as it is one of the most harmful of attacks to the one receiving the bad treatment and the one being cruel.

Usually, a cruel person is hurt more from their attitude and behavior <u>by guilt</u> than the victim of their attack. Quite a few people with emotional troubles (mental attacks) find themselves unable to concentrate well. When they read or study, their thoughts jump from one thing to another and they cannot keep them on what they are doing. With lack of concentration, you do not register what you read and then cannot recall it. This can make learning difficult (why some children with family problems at home have a hard time in school) and may affect your working efficiency--also being late for work a lot, clock watching till time to go home, dreading going to work, etc.

Another common symptom of insecurity is the inability or dislike of making decisions. If you make a decision, perhaps it will be the wrong one, so you hesitate and avoid reaching a decision or get someone else to do it for you. Fear of failure is a related matter. If you do not try, you cannot fail. Disregarded is the fact that; neither can you succeed without trying. The very word try implies failure. When you say, "I'll try," you imply that you probably will not succeed. Immaturity is another common symptom of mental attack. Much neurotic behavior and thinking is on a very immature basis. The immature person in some ways has not grown up mentally and so does not fear reality and cannot handle his or her problems in an adult, mature way. On the other hand, it would be hard to find anyone completely free of minor immaturities. Again, it is largely a matter of degree whether this is abnormal or not.

The persons who are emotionally disturbed (immature) and who have frequent psychosomatic illnesses are likely to become very self-centered. They worry about their condition, and develop a habit of being overly concerned and dwell on themselves almost continually. They are too busy thinking about themselves (selfish), even to pay much attention to the needs of others, even if those they supposedly love. Everyone has a degree of self-importance, of course, but such a person is not always considered selfish or egotistical. Some people may be very generous, if they happen to think about someone else at times, but usually they are too busy with thoughts about themselves.

I have previously mentioned psychosomatic illness and would like to conclude this letter with some explanation of this problem. Just what is a psychosomatic illness Soke? You might ask, and I will answer by defining it as an illness with the following characteristics.

1. The disorder is one of function rather than of structure, although structural changes (in the body) may occur later.
2. It is precipitated by an inadequate stimulus.
3. The response is not appropriate to the stimulus.
4. It is based on some past experience, usually painful.

Such illnesses seem to stem from problem situations and from words or thoughts rather than actual infections or injuries. Most of us realize that illness may have some psychological causes but we like to believe this is something, which may happen to others but not with us. Ours must be organic and real. If our doctor tells us that we have a psychosomatic illness, we may even resent it and find that the idea is unacceptable, at least until it is confirmed by some other physician or more.

Unfortunately, a few doctors without training in psychosomatics will feel unable to cope with such an illness and may dismiss the patient with such a remark as "It's all in your head." It may be from your emotions, but it is not just imaginary or in your head--the pain can be real. A psychologically produced pain is a mental attack and hurts just as much as an organic one (real injury). Since some of you may be familiar with the conditions, which physicians usually consider as psychosomatic, I will list just a few, to include all of them would be like printing a medical doctrine, or dictionary. With some illnesses, such as allergy and arthritis, so little is known about them that the picture is confusing. There may only be an organic basis, but usually there are psychological causes, hence I include them in my list. Some of the illnesses classified as psychosomatic are as follows. (Physical attacks caused by mental attacks.)

1. Respiratory system – Allergy, sinusitis, hay fever, common cold, bronchitis, asthma, emphysema, and pulmonary tuberculosis.
2. Skin – Eczema, urticaria, hives, and many other skin conditions, pimples, acne, i.e., dermatological conditions.
3. Digestive – Obesity, constipation, colitis, diarrhea, peptic ulcer, esophageal spasm, lack of appetite in some conditions, hemorrhoids, and gall bladder disease.
4. Vascular – High blood pressure, coronary heart disease, paroxysmal tachycardia (sudden rapid heart beat).
5. Urinary – Enuresis (bed wetting), nervous frequency, urgency, and incontinence, post-operative urinary retention.
6. Nervous system – Endocrine, migraine headache, hiccups, drug addiction, alcoholism, hyperthyroidism, diabetes mellitus, goiter, hypoglycemia.
7. Genital – MALE – Impotence, premature ejaculation, infertility. FEMALE Many menstrual disturbances, particularly dysmenorrea (cramps), infertility, habitual abortion, frigidity, leucorrea, trichomonas vaginitis, and dyspareunia.

Stress and tension may serve to lower bodily resistance so that we become more susceptible to even infectious diseases and in this sense it could be said that all illness has an emotional background. That is why we in Keichu Do are learning mental self-defense along with physical kicking, punching, blocking, etc. As you can see, mental attacks can be as dangerous, if not more so, than physical attack. Well, students, I hope you have gained some insight as you read. I will write more later.

Be as God designed you to be.

Soke Marx

Dear Mark,

I have been writing to you since 1974 my thoughts, ideas and some lectures concerning Keichu-Do, Philosophy and other areas.

Upon rediscovering the carbon copies of these letters, and with encouragement from others, I have decided to put them all together and publish a book from them. Many Keichu instructors could, hopefully, benefit from the information in these letters.

Mark, I think you will agree that it is our duty, yours and mine, to share this knowledge with others. I feel it is only fair to warn you that, "To read and not to practice what is read is folly," in this particular case at least. As you are aware, these letters are an accumulation of over sever years research on my part and much more by authors whose publications I studied. Mark, most of the problems any of us are faced with are brought on by our own thought processes. If you will recall or re-read my letters, it is possible that your memory banks would provide you with the solution to teaching what you have learned to your students.

I usually return to my notes on many occasions to aid myself when information is needed to teach a class or give a lecture. This letter will not be an instructive type but, rather, the closing for the book. Also included are some profound thoughts written by our own dear friend, Sensei Linda McCoy. I look forward to a book written by her.

Mark, I would caution you to become more aware of the inner processes going on within your own personal self. I recommend wholeheartedly that you observe the events happening in your life right now. Add the total scores of the good and not so good tallies and judge your success, imagined success and failures. If you find that your life account is in the red zone, you will then be able to recount the results, add and subtract where needed and hopefully, balance your attitude, personality and thought processes. Thus, you will be in harmony with the Universe and fine tuned to Nature. But more importantly in Gods will.

Without that end, happiness is only a shadow, and success only a temporary fantasy. I have warned you before that real success is not measured by material gain. Accomplishments are the final end of goals completed, which have worth to the individual for the betterment of mankind. That is true success. Material things are but ornaments to be displayed for ego boosting. It's fine to have material properties but not at the expense of true accomplishments.

Many truly successful persons have been misjudged and felt to be failures or losers by misconceptionists who are forever reading only the covers of books. I hope in conclusion that you my readers, have found something worth while in this book. God bless you all, and let me hear from you!

Keep Christ first in all you do.

Karl W. Marx Sr.

The Keichu Do Pledge

By

Linda McCoy

I am a student of KEICHU DO, and as such I give my pledge to do my best at all times, in the dojo and in life; to earn the respect of others by treating others with respect; to learn to lead others by first commanding myself; to be true to my Soke and the principles taught by him, and to be a faithful student to my Sensei; to bring honor to my dojo and to KEICHU DO by living with loyalty, integrity, and courage. I pledge to devote myself entirely to striving to become a whole and balanced person, physically, mentally, and spiritually.

Through the Ranks

By

Sensei Linda McCoy

It takes at least three times as long to produce a Shodan as it does a term baby. Both go through certain stages of development, which are somewhat analogous.

The dojo is like a womb; the time of training, a pregnancy. The material to be learned is like the egg cell, of which the sensei is the nucleus. There are millions of potential students "out there," but only a relative few will come into the dojo to join with the sensei to produce a new entity, a jukyu, a 10th kyu white belt. Not every fertilized egg cell becomes a baby, and not every jukyu becomes a Shodan. They both have a long way to go, and the way is often hard and even hazardous.

The white belt ranks (jukyu, kukyu, hachikyu, and shichikyu) are similar to the first few cell divisions the zygote undergoes. That is there is a lot of work being done to make a little progress. At rokkyu, sixth kyu, the student has made his first real step as he earns his yellow belt. At this stage, the zygote implants and becomes and embryo. Both have decided they're going to stick around, for a little while at least.

The dojo is the environment in which the student grows, as the child grows in the womb. The proper balance of nutrients must be supplied by the mother's body if the baby is to develop properly, and the mother must avoid passing on to the child any dangerous substances which could have an adverse effect on its development. If the Dojo environment is not properly balanced, then the "child" produced by it may not survive to term, or may survive to term but begin life with a handicap. The healthiest environment for growth is balanced in "nutrients" which are the physical, mental, and spiritual aspects of the art.

At gokyu, fifth kyu green belt, the student is really starting to grow quickly. At no other time in its development does an embryo grow so quickly as at this stage. This is the time when the student makes a real commitment to his art. If he lasts through green belt, the chances are improving that he will be able to stay until "term." It is a very critical time for student and embryo alike.

The purple belt, yonkyu (fourth kyu) student can be recognizable as a future black belt, as an embryo is recognizable as a future independent human being. It may just take a little imagination, but the resemblance and potential are there. By third kyu, sankyu, the student is clearly recognizable. The embryo is by now a fetus; it is a complete human being, but still unable to survive outside the womb. This brown belt has all the basics, but if he leaves the dojo at this time it is unlikely that he will continue on his own to grow and mature as a martial artist.

The second kyu, nikyu, brown belt is a little like a fetus at just seven months development. He has all his major parts but is still very immature. The baby who is born at this stage may or may not survive even when heroic efforts are made by others to keep him going. At first kyu, ikkyu brown belt, the chances are very good that the student will continue to grow "to term" as a martial artist. If he leaves the dojo at this point, or if he tests for black belt too soon, he could still do well but will require lots of care to do so. Although he can survive if born at this stage, the infant still needs the extra time in utero for the internal organs-- brain, lungs, digestive system--to be mature enough to cope successfully with the outside world; it may take years for this child to catch up in size and strength and maturity.

The black belt test is like labor. It comes a day that has been anticipated for a long time and prepared for with both eagerness and anxiety. That day means hours of sweat, and strain, and fatigue, and pain which can last for days afterward but is soon forgotten. But when it is finished, the world can look upon a new being—healthy, fully developed, and ready to take on the challenges of life.

The Dans, the black belt ranks, are like stages of a person's life, and indeed require and should be the remainder of ones life. As we examine these, let us keep in mind that we are discussing maturity and stage of development <u>as a black belt</u>, and the chronological age of the person involved is irrelevant. Also, let us remember that the fact of a persons reaching a certain "age" (rank) does not necessarily mean that he has reached a maturity or mental level implied by that rank. This is true in life outside the dojo as well; regrettably, many people reach a middle or even advanced age without ever attaining the maturity level implied by that age, while others are "old and wise" who have not yet attained many birthdays.

Shodan, the first year as a black belt, is similar to infancy. This student has come a long way, but still needs the loving care and attention of his parent, the sensei. The first year of Nidan is like the years of preschool and elementary school, in which the child's personality develops and the child establishes himself as an individual under the protection and guidance of the parent, although home ties can still be very strong. He tries out different ideas, concepts which may be very different from those in his own home. But if the parent is patient and strong, it is likely the child will return to the family traditions.

At Sandan, the student is like a young adult. Now a sensei in his own right, he establishes his full and mature independence from his parent, but generally maintains close family ties of affection and respect. This black belt had been as a Nidan exploring many lifestyles and deciding what is important to his needs and goals. Now as a "young adult" Sandan, he puts these things into practice in his own life and in his own home, his dojo, where he will rear "children" of his own.

Shodan, Nidan, and Sandan can be thought of as the "physical" phase of development, not because mental and spiritual development are absent but, rather, because there is more emphasis on the physical aspects of growing, maturing, and establishing.

As a Yodan, (fourth) this adult is occupied with his home and providing for his family. His ties to his parent and home of origin are never broken, although they may be less obvious now than before. He is establishing his own "family traditions" which may or may not be the same as those of his brothers and sisters. He may still think of the dojo of his parent sensei as "home," as his own children think of his dojo as "home." This phase is a transitional one, both physical and mental. The spiritual is not neglected, nor is the physical expression of the art ignored. However, the emphasis is now changing to the mental aspects of planning, interpreting, writing, supervising, and so on.

The Godan (fifth) is the mature adult who has settled into his home and his career. He is still rearing his younger children, while his older offspring are establishing themselves as adults. This parent has moved in his career into a managerial position. He may stay here until retirement, or may move up even further with the company.

The Rokudan (sixth), the wearer of the red and white belt, is now fully a master. He has earned a high managerial position in the company. His children have by now provided him with grandchildren who will themselves rear children. Like many young grandparents, he likely will be offering much advice on the rearing of these grandchildren, and if they are nearby, he may lend a hand in rearing them himself.

Godan and Rokudan can be thought of as the mental phase. Again, this is not because the physical and the spiritual are absent or neglected, but rather because duty and stage of life call for more emphasis on the mental.

By Shichidan (seventh), the master is now a top executive in the company. He is a respected grandfather and great grandfather. He has seen and supervised the passage of time and the continuance of the generations. At this point in his life, he is much less personally concerned with the infants of the family, which are several generations removed from him, although he is concerned that they carry on the family traditions correctly. Shichidan is a transitional phase, in which the emphasis is changing from the mental to the spiritual.

The Hachidan (eighth), is the great grandfather who is happy to see the new babies at the family reunions, but he bounces them on his knee and chucks them under the chin and hands them back to their parents. He is more concerned at this point that the grandparents of these new infants, who are his own grandchildren, are prepared to take over family leadership in their own turns.

The Kudan (ninth), is also concerned that their grandchildren have passed on the family's history and traditions intact. They are likely to spend very little time with anyone under "middle age," say fifth or sixth dans. Hachidan and Kudan are the stages in which the grandmaster perfects and passes down his philosophy. The eighth and ninth steps, together with the tenth, comprise the spiritual phase.

The Judan (tenth), the tenth degree wearer of the red belt, is the one and true head of the family, the ultimate authority on every question, looked to for guidance and wisdom. In spite of his great "age" (rank) and power, having the power of life and death over every household and member of the family, he has learned that true power over others is not measured by what one can force others to do, but rather it is in what others are willing to do for him of their own accord. He has learned that one can never stop learning. He does not seek to be revered for his own person, but rather has learned true humility; he does not seek to be revered for his own person, but rather has learned true humility; he does not seek to be revered but is revered, and so it should be, not for what he has become but for what he has helped others to become.

The next phase following is another transition, wherein he is changed from what we can know to what we cannot know. Perhaps he will move on farther, to another Dojo, where he will begin again. And yet part of him will always remain here, with us in what he has learned and what he has taught, and what he has passed on to his successor, who will pass it on in his turn.

This is Not Just Another Karate School
By Sensei Linda McCoy

This is not just another karate school. This is a dojo, a place for learning the way. The Way of Keichu has evolved through the years, and is always evolving. A dojo is like a temple. At first some things you will learn might seem meaningless or even silly; but if you do your best to learn them anyway, then the understanding will follow. You will learn to take pride in your dojo and in what it will come to mean to you. You will change, and as you learn to appreciate the differences in others. The more you learn, the more you will discover there is to learn. Don't become discouraged. Remember that "half of being smart is knowing what you're dumb at." Respect this place because of the learning that takes place here. You are now a part of this place, and it will become a part of you.

This is not just another karate school. It is the home of your Sensei. Of course, not many teachers actually live in their dojo any more, but long ago the only dojos were the homes of the teachers. Teaching was not available to large numbers of the public but, rather, was limited to only a few selected students who lived with the instructor as though they were his sons. Even in recent years, students were admitted to the dojo only on the highest recommendations and after careful scrutiny of their moral character, after which they waited perhaps years and passed very exciting tests to prove their worthiness. Just as you reserve the right to invite into your home only certain people, the sensei also has the right to refuse to admit to the dojo anyone at any time for any reason.

This is not just another karate school. This is my heart I share with you. You have come to me because you want to learn what I can teach you. By allowing you to become part of my dojo, I have accepted the responsibility of teaching you what you need to know. By becoming part of my dojo, you are accepting the responsibility to learn what I have to teach, and I have a lot more to teach than just kick and punch. The money you give to me is not payment for lessons but is merely something that allows me to provide for a place for us to meet. It does not give you the right to tell me what to teach or how to teach it. If you have a problem with what I teach, come to me and we will talk it over together. I am not out to get rich teaching karate. I am here to share with you my way of life; there is no way you can buy that.

This is not just another karate school. This is not just a class, it's a family. As this is my house, all of you are my children. I expect that in spite of the disagreements that will always crop us in any family, that we will come to respect each other and even come to love one another, even if we don't always like each other. The sensei is the head of the household, and as such is the ultimate authority on every question. The sensei's word is law, but that is not to imply an unwillingness to discuss all sides of any matter. This dojo is a household, and is related to other households with whom we share the family name of Keichu, and a common way of life.

This is not just another karate school. This is a Keichu-Do dojo. Keichu means "devoting oneself entirely"--not to your sensei or to your dojo, but to the way of life we share. Devoting yourself entirely will mean doing your best at everything, all the time--at school, at work, at home, in the dojo--so that you can become the person you want to be.

135

An Extra Lagniappe From a Cajun Master & Bayou Boy

WHAT'S WITH THAT?

Many of you readers might not agree with me, however just because YOU don't believe what I say, doesn't mean that I am wrong. It just might be YOU who are mistaken. I'm open minded, show me your proof and I'll really consider changing MY mind. My question today is why are men and women so often at war with each other? What's with that?

In the old days it was the bridegroom who was the big deal at the wedding. The bride to be waited, not knowing when her beloved would arrive. Read it yourself, it's in the Bible, for sure yeah. These days it's the bride who keeps the groom waiting at the altar, and every body stands when SHE enters. There has always been a stinking double standard between the sexes with the man for the most part being a dictator, chauvinist pig, who treats wives terribly. That was not God's will. God taught us that a man should love his wife as much as he loved himself.

What's with this system we (or should I say some men) have today? The man asks a girl out for dinner, and in many cases he has to wait 15 or so minutes for her to get ready. He opens the doors for her (if he is a gentleman) every where they go, at the car, the restaurant, pulls the chair out for her to sit, stands up when she has to go to the ladies room, doggone it! The man act's like a cotton picking door man at a ritzy place. The man pays for the movies, for dinner, or breakfast. He buys her presents, treats her so nice, UNTIL he beds her or weds her. Then, in too many cases, he begins to treat his love mate with disrespect, disdain and takes her for granted. "What's with that?"

The sayings that "Girls just want what they can't have," and "Guys just want what they never had" appear to have some legitimacy when one sees what the world has come to. People of today appear to be shopping for a mate the way they shop to buy a car. They want to "TRY IT OUT" first.

Couples starts out in sin, by fornicating out of wedlock and then wonder why God is not happy with them. Then when their relationship goes sour or their marriage hits the rocks, they blame each other and God. What does God have to do with that? It is their choice to have sex before marriage; Got is not with that. However, when anyone messes up and the results are not to their liking, they usually blame God. You drink too much, get drunk and decide to drive home. Your friends attempt to drive you home but you won't have it. So you have an accident and cuss God. Why? What's with that? Think about this.

DID YOU KNOW?

Hi Ho every body! Yes, it's me the old blabbermouth, with the razor sharp tongue, the uncouth, rude, and in –your-face attitude. I'm generally an all around Bible thumping, hand-raising, Spirit-filled, moved, and led, born again, Blessed and SAVED by the Blood of Jesus Christ, Pastor of a martial art outreach Ministry. Wow! That's a mouth full. I have another mouth full to share with all of you, my faithful readers. Like the Prophets of old it is my duty to inform the world of the utter shortness of their salvation at this present time. The idea of not thinking about the shortness of our lifetime, nevertheless doesn't add to it. Any of us could go at any given moment, Cheesh! Not that we should go all the time worrying about dying, that would be ludicrous.

The truth be known, however, is that any one without their ticket cannot board the Plane to Heaven. Jesus Christ on the Cross-has already paid for the ticket. He gave His life for ours. He took the bullet for you and me, if you get my drift. Making plans for the future is not bad. It is just unwise to count your chickens before the eggs hatch. I learned a long time ago that whereas we do not know what will happen tomorrow. Hay! For what is life? It is like a vapor that appears for a little time and then vanishes away. We should think instead that if the Lord wills, we shall and do this or that. Too many folks just never believe that their number could be up at any given moment. I would imagine that not many victims of Death's coming ever knew that they would die at any given time. Surprise! Guess who's here? RIGHT! The Grim Reaper. Did you know, now it's too late for you to repent for all your sins. Busted is a nice term for what will happen, and the fine is all that are busted without Christ as Savior.

So that is why no one should be caught unaware of their position in their walk with Almighty God. Baby! You had better be in sync, walk the line, ha! This is a walk the walk, as well as a talk the talk situation. Dear ones, if YOU are not a believer, consider this, as a fair warning. GET A LIFE! It's not a question of "Got Milk?" The truth is "GOT JESUS?" Without Jesus Christ there is NO LIFE! Only an existence. Jesus said HE was the Way, the Truth, and the Life. Are you getting this yet? No intelligent person will play Russian roulette with a derringer pistol. After all, only an idiot would take a 50/50 chance like that. Think of it this way. Either I'm right or I'm wrong. OK! If I'm wrong I lose nothing, except a lot of drunken parties, my head in a toilet throwing up, my insides out, a bad headache the next day, fights over some other fellow's girlfriend, wife or daughter.

If you abuse your body like that, it will end up in the same terrible shape mine is in now, because of the stupid way I lived before I came to know Jesus. When I was a young stag of 28 years, my body was so worn out from abusing drugs (speed) mostly and Wild Turkey, Calvert, and Scotch on the rocks, that I had the body of a 68-year old man. Now if I'm right, and I believe I am with all my heart and soul, then you, all who are living without Christ as your Savior and best friend, are in for a horrible future. You don't really want to go there. You have never experienced real pain, and sorrow, like what awaits you. Snakebite would be a pleasure compared to some of the things you will experience. Am I trying to scare you? Yes, I am. I hope to scare the living Hell out of you, and then the Devil will not have YOUR human body to house in.

What's keeping any of you from accepting Jesus Christ as your Savior? Come on! What? Pride? Simple plain old over blown egos - pride, is the culprit here. That is the FIRST sin ever committed. Lucifer the most beautiful angel in Heaven at that time became proud of his position, and declared his infamous five I's: "I will ascend into heaven." "I will exalt MY throne above the stars of God." That wasn't too smart. "I will also sit on the mount of the congregation" Oh, man and there was more! "I will ascend above the heights of the clouds" Yea! Right. "I WILL BE like the Most High." And that cut it! WRONG! Hay! Can I have an AMEN! Here? HA! Sounds a little like preaching to me. Oh! Dear God, I should be so blessed, to serve in that manner. Well, The Word is out, man, it's already confirmed, cut in stone, measured and set. God Himself has promised to punish the fruit of the arrogant heart. Ouch! It's true too, because I have experienced that punishment for my pride.

When any of us claim to be what we are not, so we can feel better about ourselves, we are liars and deceivers. God said in Isaiah 10:10 "Woe to those who decree unrighteous decrees." Just that alone is a BIG RED Light. I'm a 10th Dan is a mighty huge statement. That statement is definitely a decree, and in most of today's claims a proven unrighteous decree. (God's going to get YOU for that.) Are there any real 10th Dans living in this day and age? I think so. However, who promotes them to that rank and what are the requirements? Just because someone is the founder of a self-made style doesn't qualify him or her to be a 10th Dan. The more we brag on ourselves to build our esteem higher, the deeper we bury ourselves away from God. Hay! The Lord of Hosts (GOD) musters the army for battle. I don't know about you, brother, but as for me and my house we will serve the Lord. God is MY salvation.

Right! You know were I stand, how about you? Write me, argue if you must, but the truth is the truth. Now don't insult my intelligence with trite pact old crap answers, like "well the truth for me might not be the truth for you." LAME! The truth is never changing. It is true for you and true for me. Jesus Christ is the Truth. Come on folks, GET A GRIP! Your time could be up before you finish reading this message. I am not attempting to be a hard case here, OK? I merely wish to invite you to the biggest, and best Party of ALL TIME. In Heaven, later Gator.

Habitual Christianity

Habitual Christianity...is that possible? What would that include? This question is about something as dangerous to Christians as stepping on a rusty nail. I wonder how many and if I myself don't slip into this terrible situation. God forbid, but then how does one know if what and how they are conducting themselves is habitual or not. Do you go to church every Sunday because you just can't get enough of God's Word, or do you go because you are expected to be there? I wonder sometimes if the deeper we get into Church duties, like becoming a deacon or elder, our attendance depends on how we really feel or how we are expected to feel.

The thought of my becoming habitual for any reason sends shivers down my spine. I want to feel like going out to one of the best restaurants in the world and eating a seven-course meal, when I'm going to Church. The Word of God should be looked forward to with at least equal enthusiasm. I remember when I was a Catholic, saying the Rosary was quite relaxing to me, so much so that I would fall asleep a lot while saying the Hail Mary, but then I often fall asleep these days in Church, I've been called the "Sleeping Deacon." I sometimes fall asleep while talking to someone, or driving down the road. That could be fatal. Do you remember how you feel when you were going to the movie you had waited two months to see? How about going to a ball game? You know how worked up you get. Well, going to hear God speaking should be even more exciting!!

I fear too many folks just take Church for granted and fail to really get into the soul of Church. Talk about some dull brains. All too many people are so stingy that they tip a waitress 15% for a meal, yet will not even give the Lord even

144

10% of their wages.   Can you imagine putting one dollar into the collection plate? Now this is not concerning the very poor individual. I am talking about the fellow who thinks he or she cannot afford to give 10% to their Church; they yet will spend five times that amount on beer or cigarettes. Habitual Christianity is always going to Church, sitting in the same spot all the time, and zoning out in a daydream of fishing or golfing and not paying attention while the preacher is delivering his sermon/message. A lot of people just go to Church, and then leave often before the last song so they don't have to talk to anyone. No Fellowship at all.   What's with that?

Printed in the United States
17288LVS00005B/331-339